# Thanks, Santa,
## But Who's Gonna Put It Together?

# Thanks, Santa,
## But Who's Gonna Put It Together?

## Owen Canfield

ACTEX Publications, Inc.
Winsted, Connecticut

Manufactured in the United States of America

10 9 8 7 6 5 4 3 2 1

Cover Design by T-Square Advertising and Design

Library of Congress Cataloging-in-Publication Data

Canfield, Owen, 1934-
   Thanks, Santa, but who's gonna put it together? / Owen Canfield.
      p. cm.
   Collection of the author's Christmas columns which originally appeared in the Hartford Courant, 1965-1994.
      ISBN 1-56698-192-1
   1. Canfield, Owen, 1934-   . 2. Journalists--United States--20th century--Biography. 3. Christmas--Humor. I. Title.
PN4874.C235A3   1995
070'.92--dc20
[B]                                    95-45542
                                          CIP

ISBN: 1-56698-192-1

# Contents

# Acknowledgments

Most of the material appearing in this book was originally published in *The Hartford Courant*. It is reprinted and published here by permission of *The Courant*.

The author and publisher most gratefully acknowledge the kindness of *The Hartford Courant* in making possible the publication of this work.

To Ethel and the Gallant Ten

# Thanks, Santa,
## But Who's Gonna Put It Together?

Ethel and I had been married for six and one-half months, and our honeymoon was still going on, when Christmas arrived in 1955. Because the holiday would become the celebration which would forever define us as a family, 40 years have not dimmed the memory of that first quiet Christmas in the South.

I was 21, Ethel 10 months older. If we had a problem, it was her complaint that, while we had been married more than half a year, she was not yet pregnant.

"I want a miniature," she often said. I distinctly remember she said it that day, 6½ months into our marriage, little realizing that, within 6½ years, she would have seven "miniatures," with three more to come.

We missed the snow and cold weather, but Alexandria, Louisiana, my last post before discharge from the U.S. Air Force, offered nothing in the way of winter beyond a few chilly mornings.

We bought a two-foot high artificial tree, placed it on an end table in our small apartment, and decorated it. On Christmas morning, after walking to Mass at nearby Our Lady of Prompt Succor Catholic Church, we exchanged a couple of inexpensive gifts. Later, she prepared a fine dinner and we called my parents in Torrington, Connecticut.

During the previous year, when I served in Korea, we had written each other every day and discovered that we did indeed love each other. Our first six months of marriage had revealed, unquestionably (and perhaps even more importantly), that we liked each other as well. We were well-matched, laughed a lot, and always put each other first.

"Next year," she said, "we'll be home with the family."

Ethel had been born near Newcastle-on-Tyne in England, and orphaned during World War II. At age 7, she found herself at Fairbridge Farm School on Vancouver Island in British Columbia.

In this orphanage she grew up with about 100 other children of similar circumstances. At 16, she "went out" to live as a housekeeper and governess to Rick and Mary

Burgess, the young children of Jack and Joan Burgess of Victoria. Jack and Joan became her guardians and were kind and good to her. But at 19, in 1952, at Joan's urging, she joined the Royal Canadian Air Force.

We met in late 1953 when I was stationed in St. Albans, Vermont, and she was stationed at Lac St. Denis, Quebec, some 50 miles above Montreal. We had known each other only three months when I shipped out for Korea, but before I left I was able to take her to meet my folks in Connecticut. They embraced her immediately.

Ethel and me just before Christmas, 1953, on her first visit to my family in Torrington.

My mother and father, brother, and two sisters swiftly became as much Ethel's family as they were mine. We spent Christmas with them that year. By the time I brought her to the Hartford railroad station to catch the Montrealer back to her base in early January, she had captured their affections as she had mine.

Half a dozen times during 1954 Ethel, on three-day breaks, made her way from Lac St. Denis to Montreal and rode the Washingtonian from Montreal to Hartford, where my father and mother would pick her up. They enjoyed her visits as much as she did.

In 1954, now for all practical purposes one of their daughters, she spent Christmas with them. She told me later that it was the happiest Christmas of her life to that time.

I arrived home in February of 1955 and we married in May. Now here we were, celebrating our first Christmas together by a two-foot tree, homesick but happy with each other and with what we felt would surely be a grand future.

Ethel Riley,
RCAF, 1953

Owen Canfield,
USAF, 1953

# Nineteen Sixty-Five

*I came to journalism at age 26 without an hour of college credit. Trusting my enthusiasm,* The Torrington Register *took me on in July 1960.  I resigned from my job as a milkman, put on a necktie, and began a newspaper career that would last over 35 years.*

*Ethel, who had encouraged me through a year-long correspondence course in fiction and article writing paid for by the GI Bill, was also pleased but could give her approval only after I promised to get a part-time job to make up for the $15 per week pay cut I had to take.  The* Register *paid $60 per week, to start.*

*Oh, yes, there were miniatures by now. Linda had been born in July 1957, Sheila in September 1958, and Owen on Christmas Day of 1959.  Moreover, we were expecting another baby here in December of 1960.*

*We missed a second consecutive Christmas birth by a few hours. We didn't know there were twins on the way until Kathy arrived some 20 minutes after Kevin. In those days, you didn't always know. Steven and Sharon came*

*along together in April 1962. Again, we were surprised to find our number increased by two without warning.*

*In 1962, with a GI loan, no down payment, and a 30-year mortgage, we bought the 10-room house we had rented five years earlier.*

Christmas Eve, 1960. Ethel holds Owen. I have Sheila, left, and Linda.

*Tricia was born in December 1964, beating Christmas by 2½ weeks. In September 1965, I joined the sportswriting staff at* The Hartford Courant, *and on Christmas Day my first* Courant *column appeared.*

*At the* Register, *I had often written columns about the kids and Ethel. Before my first* Courant *column, I asked assistant sports editor Bill Newell if it would be permissible to do the same here in Hartford, since it would appear on Christmas Day.*

*"Sure," he said. "A good column is a good column anywhere."*

*Thrilled and excited, I spent hours writing my first* Courant *column.*

*The column worked. Response was positive. Christmas of 1964 was my subject, and Ethel's authoritative role in family management was the theme.*

When winter replaced fall, it stood to reason we had to play football in the house. In photo above, fall was still with us. Owen holds the football. Sheila and Linda stand with Kathy and Kevin on the swings.

# Grist from the Sports Mill

**December 25, 1965**

Christmas morning, and it's so quiet you can hear a strip of tinsel hit the rug. The tree glows in the pre-dawn stillness, and in the soft light of many-colored bulbs, you don't notice the lower branches are overburdened, out of balance with the almost barren upper portion.

In daylight, you can tell kids did the trimming.

Ma and I just finished arranging things under the tree. She's asleep in a chair. There was no use going to bed. It's almost time for things to break loose. Pretty soon the sun will eat up the night and that's the signal. I'm ready to drop off but I'm hanging on.

I had to wait for Ma to doze to slip the last present under the tree. I buried the football at the bottom, in the back, so by the time it's discovered there'll be enough excitement, I hope, so she won't notice right away.

Ma doesn't like football, because of last Christmas. I remember it like it was 10 minutes ago, foggy as my mind is right now.

Funny about Ma. A year ago at this time, she could tolerate the pigskin game. We sat right here at just about this time of morning, talking about how the boys would enjoy their new ball and helmets, with me filling her full of how I could teach them to pass and run plays, and so on, with a good ball rather than the little rubber thing they were then using. I remember stressing the importance of proper equipment with kids of five, four, and three. It must have sounded reasonable, because she agreed then.

The room looks nice, like the scene on a Christmas card, but if things go like last year, and I'm determined they won't, a few hours will turn it into what any Red Cross or Federal expert in the business would classify a disaster area on sight.

I know what's coming because I went through it last year, but this year I'm ready. There's no doubt that the hidden football, if thrown or kicked with any force, could lay that tree out cold, but I'm not going to let it happen. Not this year.

Trouble with giving footballs just as the football season is ending, is that the snow keeps you off the yard. If you're going to play, you're going to play inside. And if you've got a new football, you're going to play.

Last year the boys didn't pay much attention to the ball until about mid-morning, when the batteries ran down on a few remote control things. They donned their helmets and began a game, using the hall and an adjoining room. I got in just to make it even, two against two. Owen and I took on Kevin and Steven. The game lasted one play and Ma began disliking football right then and there. It's painfully clear in my mind.

I huddled with Owen. "Go down to the TV set and cut toward the couch, but block Kevin first," I instructed. It was a busted play. He centered from the doorway, but the ball bounced in front of me and Kevin, offside by a mile, charged by him just prior to the snap, so he missed the block. Steven didn't know much about the defensive secondary so he followed his brother in. They were on top of me before I could straighten up, but I scooped up the ball and backpedalled. I wanted to scramble, but there was neither time nor room.

I let fly a desperate pass. Owen was in the clear, but the pass was overthrown. The hall was clogged with miscellaneous toys. A wooden truck tripped me up and I crashed backward, cracking my head sharply on a small table. The two attackers landed on my stomach, knocking my wind out with a whoosh. Kevin's helmet chocked against my jaw and I bit my tongue.

The defensive team laughed hilariously and rolled off.

The ace receiver, meanwhile, had troubles of his own. Racing for the ball, he ran through the designated end zone and into the next room, where new disaster loomed. The two little girls and the two big girls had just set up housekeeping with their new dolls. Keeping his eye on the ball, as any receiver worth his salt would, he didn't see the doll house, and even if he had, he couldn't have stopped. He landed on it and it collapsed a floor at a time, like a book closing, and little chairs and beds flew everywhere. His helmet saved him from possible head injuries.

In the hall, I was dazed and holding my head. Blood was running freely from a sizable gash at the back. My tongue, I felt, was now only half a tongue. The two little girls, their doll house wrecked and furniture scattered, howled a tearful protest, and the big girls shrieked with rage. Kevin and Steven, amused and interested, stood quietly for a moment looking down at me. Owen sat on the misshapen doll house roof, disappointed at the inaccuracy of the pass. The baby began to cry upstairs. Ma ran in with a cold cloth for my head and then picked up the football and put it high on the refrigerator.

One play.

It took all afternoon to straighten and repair the doll house. I still get occasional headaches. Ma's enthusiasm for football steadily faded after that.

The football? We haven't seen it for a while, though it had an interesting, if expensive, life in this house before disappearing. Kept me in shape, not only throwing it around with the boys, but retrieving it from trees, the garage roof, under the porch, and other places.

It also broke one window pane and cracked another, popped three light bulbs, and, one pleasant fall day, swept a coconut layer cake off a picnic table in the back yard as neat as a whistle.

Nobody can remember where he last saw the football. The boys always kept it in their room with the helmets. Ma just shakes her head, apparently having no knowledge of its whereabouts.

She never seemed to like it anyway, probably because it caused all that trouble last Christmas. Not that I'm accusing her of anything.

The new one, now, she's bound to go for. It's junior size and the boys will be able to handle it. It's a first class ball. I know you can kick it a mile because I tried it out Saturday when everybody was downtown.

The boys are a year older now, I'll point out when the new football is found and Ma points the accusing finger. Besides, what's Christmas without a ball? There won't be any more playing in the house, I'll promise. (And if we do have a little game today, just going through the motions, we'll make sure the hall is clear and nobody will get in trouble.) What good are helmets without a ball, I'll ask her. This junior-sized ball will be no problem to center, I'll add, and remind her that a bad snap caused all the commotion last year and it can't happen again with this ball. Actually, I've got all kinds of arguments going for me.

I'll just observe and referee. What can go wrong? There will be no contact and no running. She can't get mad over a football on Christmas morning, can she?

It's been over a month since the other ball turned up missing and I'll be honest, the boys have missed it. I say it's not fair. The way I feel, boys who enjoy playing should have a football. She's sure to see it that way, isn't she?

I'm dying to try that pass play we saw in the Giants game last week, where Meredith flipped to Hayes on the sideline and he went all the way.

If I stand on the edge of the rug and just toss ever so easily to Owen near the radiator — ah, perfect. Steven can center and Kevin will take Jimmy Patton's part. I can see it now. How can you get in any trouble when things are organized like that?

# Nineteen Seventy-One

*Six years had elapsed since my first Christmas column, and we were now a full complement of 12 people. Linda, the oldest, was 14 years old and a freshman in high school. Maureen had been born in March 1966 and Daniel, the baby, now almost 4, in January 1968, ten years and six months after Linda.*

*Ethel's unspoken Christmas "rules" were by now established and observance of them was routine. The seven-and-a-half-foot tree was erected three days before the holiday, in the southeast corner of the living room. It was decorated by all of us, after I had clipped the lights to the branches and placed the plastic angel at the top.*

*We purchased two dozen donuts on Christmas Eve. On Christmas morning, the children rose early and dressed in their best clothes. They were allowed to gaze at the tree and the bounty Santa Claus had left, but not to touch until we had attended 7 a.m. Mass, returned home, and consumed a donut and orange juice. The tension was almost unbearable, but all of us were able to restrain ourselves while the ritual played out.*

*The children seated themselves around the room, little ones often pairing up with older ones so that they could have help removing wrapping paper, when their time came.*

*It was my job to pass the gifts to each child, Ethel, and myself. Each child received five gifts, plus the little things, including sweet treats, which filled the large stockings. Then we opened them one at a time, going around the room. This done, it was play time.*

*Sports had a high priority in our house, and sports equipment always found its way under our Christmas trees. I could never resist helping the boys try out their new gifts.*

Sharon, Kathy, Linda, and Sheila. Christmas dolls. Ethel, peeking around the corner. She knit a Christmas stocking, like those in the background, for each child.

# Trying Out the Equipment

**December 25, 1971**

The season to be jolly reaches ground zero today. Why, then, am I apprehensive?

I'm not by nature a pessimistic man, yet Christmas Day finds me concerned with intangibles and gripped by uncertainty.

In a few minutes, I will be called on to officiate at tree-side ceremonies at which yon mountain of presents will be dispensed and stacked in 10 little mountains, each guarded by its owner.

There will be six female guards and four male guards. The girls do not disturb me. Their packages contain no threat to my well-being.

The boys are another story. There is potential dynamite lurking beneath that sheep's-clothing wrapping paper. This is a sports house, and sports equipment of one denomination or another finds its way beneath our tree every December 25.

When the wrappers are off, and the 10 little mountains have been decimated, the trying out begins.

Girls can try their new gifts forever, and never cause a nerve ripple.

Boys can't. Sports equipment demands to be tested properly, and in the true spirit of its physical nature.

Let's go back six years, when the big mountain was broken down only eight ways, with three guarded by boys.

That Christmas is remembered in our house for a midget-sized baseball bat, wielded forcefully in the midget-sized hands of its new owner.

The bat was an eleventh hour addition, picked up in the very last store we hit on our very last day of shopping, December 24.

It looked like a Nellie Fox bottle bat, only half-size, and it caught my eye as we approached the cashier's counter. "Perfect for Steven," I observed.

"He's got enough. We don't need it," warned Ma.

We bought the bat, which was cute for a little kid, and all wood. Believe me it was solid wood, through and through.

He tried it out that afternoon in a wide open space in the front room. His brother, being older, obligingly pitched to him, using a plastic ball that couldn't possibly break anything even if Willie Stargell tagged it right on the nose.

I strolled in to study the kid's swing at the wrong moment. Precisely the wrong moment. I was tired. I wasn't careful. He was swinging as I was walking and he connected.

Now, in cold weather, my leg, just below the knee, has a tendency to ache. I remember blinding pain as bottle bat and shin came together, I remember not being able to talk for a while, and I remember not being allowed to say what I wanted and, I still feel, had every right to say when my articulation returned.

"It's Christmas," said Ma, and I was done for before I could find my voice.

A year or two later we tried out a new football. We passed the pigskin back and fourth and then we had to run a few plays, and pretty soon we had a little game going — two-hand touch, so nobody would get hurt.

The game ended on the first play when the only defensive back on the "field" backpeddled expertly but foolishly, tripped and fell on a tin doll house. He smashed the thing into unrecognizable wreckage, and we spent the rest of the day trying to resurrect it. We wound up buying a new one on December 26.

The next year everybody got ice skates and tried them out. That was the day I found out I'd never be a hockey player. An eight-year-old boy raced me across the pond and beat me by 20 yards.

"I let you win," I told him.

"Sure you did," he answered, and I remember thinking he was pretty much of a smart-aleck, for eight.

Last year we got a new basketball and . . . well, I think you've got the idea.

You can understand the reason for my apprehension, but here's the funny part:  in an hour this feeling will be gone, completely forgotten, as if it never existed. Anticipation will supplant it.

Strange, but it happens every year.  My wife says I worry too much anyway.

# Nineteen Seventy-Three

*Crises were common but we were able to handle most of them without trouble. Ethel was calm and very cool under pressure. In the summer of 1972, Maureen, then 6, was hit by a car in front of our house and seriously injured. Quick work by the Torrington Police Department's emergency unit and by the Doctors Thomas Danaher, father and son, surgeons at Charlotte Hungerford Hospital, saved her life and she mended quickly.*

*The incident reminded us that some things were out of our hands and taught all of us to appreciate each other a little more.*

*The kids knew our financial limitations. They worked hard as soon as they were able to earn their own spending money. The older ones provided a good example for their younger siblings.   Ethel and I also worked to instill a sense of responsibility that would come in handy in later years.*

*The years flew by.   On Christmas Day of 1973, I used my* Courant *column to look back fondly on things that had gone before and to take note of how quickly the years were passing.*

The big girls with their mother, 1973.

# Ghosts of Christmas Past

**December 25, 1973**

Things are changing around here, and it's about time. This Christmas will be the most peaceful in this house in a dozen years.

Everybody's growing up. It figures that three little kids don't cause as much commotion as eight, or nine, or ten little kids, so this will be a comparatively quiet Christmas.

The big kids range in age from 16 to 11. More help than hinderance. No problem.

This is the first year I can remember in a decade that I've only had to put the Christmas tree up once. The all-time record is five, established in 1966. I finally nailed that ragged fir to the wall and braced it with 2-by-4's.

This tree, the one I'm looking at right now, looks good. Meticulously decorated and artistically lighted. What the little kids fouled up in the pre-bedtime decoration ceremony, the big kids redressed after they went to bed. I never had an eye for it as they have.

It's great, though, all this beforehand preparation. Our gifts have been wrapped for days, unlike when the kids were little.  In Christmases past, the night before was a race with the clock.

It was work all night and hope you make it.  Keep one eye on the stairs or you'll be nabbed red-handed.

Christmas Eves past are hazy memories of miles of wrapping paper and Scotch tape. Run to the cellar ... run to the closet ... check everywhere ... don't miss anything ... fill the stockings ... keep your eye on the stairs ... turn down the radio ... talk in a whisper.  Are those footsteps? Quick, head him off.  Coffee?  Thanks, I need it.  Keep working ... we can't be tired tonight ... put this fire truck together ... let's have a coffee.

Hectic.

Thank heavens, that's over.  I'll bet we don't have an hour's work tonight.  All there is to do is spread the presents under that very proper Christmas tree.

Then, fill the stockings and get a night's sleep.

At last.  Think of it.  A night's sleep on Christmas Eve.

This Christmas won't be like 1959, when Ma and I helped two little girls open their presents and then she looked at me and said, "Let's go."

I said, "Where?"

She said, "To the hospital".   And my Christmas present that year was a son.

And it won't be like 1960, when we helped two little girls and their little brother open their presents, and then Ma just looked at me — didn't say anything — and I said, "Let's go."

My present that year was another son, and a daughter, both coming a day after Christmas.

Those five, and the five who have come along since, make Christmas a pretty special day around here.

Of course, I have dark memories of the Christmas of 1967.  Who wouldn't?  That was the year of ice skates, and we went, that very day, to the frozen pond, they to try out their new blades, me to show them how.

After they skated around and past me for an hour or so, they talked me into a race across the pond.  It was the most embarrassing day of my life.   There were other people there, and I finished dead last.  I also tore a gaping hole in the seat of a new pair of trousers when I fell on a branch that had frozen into the ice.

They were infuriatingly sympathetic.  When it was ascertained that I wasn't physically incapacitated, they all smiled those superior smiles and skated away, as if to say, "I don't know this guy."

It's good to know I won't have to go through anything like that again.

There's a basketball under this proper tree this year, as there usually is. Sports equipment has always been given priority. But I doubt I'll get my hands on this one. The boys have moves I can't cope with anymore. I'm still taller and bigger than they are, but I can't run with them. When I try, it just doesn't work out. They beat me to the hoop. Not like it used to be, I can tell you. Except for an occasional game of long and short, I'm strictly a spectator or a referee, which is great, because it gives me more time to myself, which I never had before.

Of course, Daniel looks to me for guidance in sports. He's almost six. When his brothers aren't around, he comes to me to have a catch and ask questions about Butkus, and Page, and Griese, his favorite football players. His brothers, though, one or the other, are usually around, come to think of it.

That's the way it should be, too.

Well, it's time to start laying things out under that carefully trimmed tree. Everything's quiet. Everything's wrapped. Ma's working on the stockings already. It won't even take an hour.

All the teenagers put their gifts down before they went to bed. And the big girls helped the little ones wrap their things, and read "The Night Before Christmas" to

them before putting them to bed.  That used to be my job.
Well, again, less for Ma and me to do.

You know, I'll probably sit up all night even though
I don't have to.  For years I yearned for sleep on this
night, and now that I can get it, I'm not the least bit
fatigued.  Strange how things work.

I think I'll ask Ma to put on the coffee, when we're
through here, and just sit and look at that very proper tree.
And if we hear footsteps, it will be an easy matter to head
off the eager beaver, because we're just sitting here with
nothing to do but wait.

Lord, how things are changing around here.  People
are growing up.

Fast.

Too fast.

And I don't like it one little bit.

 # Nineteen Seventy-Five

*I'm not handy. I can paint walls, ceilings, and clapboards, lift heavy things, chop wood, and move furniture around. Please don't ask me why your car is making a strange noise or what is wrong with your furnace.*

*I was able to write well enough to hold the* Courant *job I loved. But a handyman I was not. "Good thing you can write, Owen," Ethel would joke cold-bloodedly after observing one of my profanity-filled bouts with a leaky sink or broken light fixture, "Because you sure can't do anything else."*

*My incompetence as a handyman extended to Christmas trees. They would tell you that if they could talk, and in my 1975 column, I pretended that they could.*

# I Never Met a Christmas Tree I Didn't Like

**December 25, 1975**

I admit I have no patience. I admit that after 17 years of dragging puffy, prickly Christmas trees through that door and into this living room, and wrestling them upright in that corner, I should be skilled in the art (and it is an art — not the trimming, just the putting up, for me).

But Christmas trees, it seems, are my natural enemies, or used to be. The sixties are remembered, around here, for epic, running battles between man and evergreen; costly battles that would last sometimes for days and extract major casualties to body and spirit.

The first few years, 1958 to 1961, produced only skirmishes. Putting up the tree was nothing dangerous. Balance was the key. Once up, the tree would stay up. There were only four or five of us at that time. Nothing more exciting than a fallen bauble ever happened. Tame stuff.

And that's the way it is now. It's come full circle. Last couple of years, no pitched battles, and hardly a problem. Once a tree is up, up it stays.

The decade of Christmases which began in 1962 was a decade of matching wits with the evergreen enemy and the law of gravity. Heroism? I don't claim that. Old fashioned, All-American, Buckle-Down-Winsocky perseverance? Yes. Definitely, because for 10 years I had to put up every Christmas tree at least twice.

If those 10 trees could come together in some Christmas Tree Valhalla, wherever dead Christmas trees go, they would tell of their experiences — making me the aggressor, the antagonist. THEY would claim heroism.

Like old soldiers at a reunion, they'd unfold their slanted stories of Christmas campaigns hard won.

I can hear them now...

Hero of '62: "I didn't like his attitude from the start. Sawed off the bottom of my trunk, he did, and straightaway I vowed to get even. He dragged me in the house and I reached out and caught myself around the porch railing just for spite. Well sir, he got me up solid, without braces or anything. Just standing flat on the floor. Pretty soon, he comes back with his wife and five little kids come in and begin with the trimmin'. I want you to know my arms were tired when they finished, since none but him and the wife could reach very high, and my lower branches had to bear the bulk of the burden. Well, I waited 'till they all stepped back to admire me. By this time he's in good spirits and tellin' himself what a good job *he'd* done."

"Then I start to lean. The wife smiles an apprehensive smile and warns, 'It's listing to port.' Too late, of course. He turns and jumps toward me but I'm gone by then. I tell you boys, it must have been a comical thing to see, judging from the laughter of the wife and kids, but *he* didn't think so. You never heard such language. He stands me back up, they rearrange things on my branches, and the last thing I remember is the wife saying, 'You're not putting those spikes in MY floor!'"

Hero of 1963: "There were seven kids when I got there. Sneakylike, he tied me up with red yarn so I couldn't fall. I played it smart, though. The day before Christmas, a couple of the boys came by and stood there, daring each other to climb me. 'Course, I egged 'em on and sure enough, they couldn't resist it. One crawled under and started up. I tried to brace, you know, and let him get a good hold. Then, whang, that yarn snapped like spaghetti, and I just laid right down in a hurry, let me tell you. The lady called him up at work. 'Disaster area,' she said. He charged in a few minutes later and ruined a good pair of pants puttin' me up again."

A brave, if scraggly, tree and Plaster Paint, who would distinguish himself by giving years of noble service, 1963

Hero of 1964: "There were eight kids then, so you can see the possibilities. I'd been standing for days, anchored with a double strand of yarn. Thought my chance would never come.

'Til Christmas eve. I saw *him* putting together this red fire truck. Took him three hours, and then *he* didn't get it right. Next morning, that fire truck got a workout. Two boys racing around the house, puttin' out imaginary fires. I knew what was comin'. Finally, down the hall they came, a streak of red, with one drivin' and one on the back — right at me. They tried a last-second turn into an armchair. No way. Too late. They hit me amidships and the crash shook the house. Shook *him* too, right out of his shoes. Christmas decorations flew to all points of the room. There was tinsel on the television set and the angel on my head landed on the couch. Those two scamps picked themselves up, hauled their truck out of the mess and were off again. He had a nervous breakdown, right there. Swear he did."

Oh, sure. These heroic Christmas trees, in their Valhalla, would have a million laughs boasting of how they had beaten me by refusing to stand up and look pretty, the way traditional trees are expected to. The Hero of '66 would lay claim to the record, having come crashing to the floor a total of five times, twice before Christmas, once Christmas Day, and twice after Christmas.

He would be toasted by his compatriots.

Old '68 would tell of catching a new basketball right in the breadbasket (wherever a Christmas tree's breadbasket may be), shaking needles loose and doing a swan dive over a surprised baby. I can hear them all chuckling and chortling and patting each other on the backs (wherever a Christmas tree's back may be).

But I honestly say that no tree ever got the best of me — that every fall was followed by swift, if chaotic, reconstruction. Battles I lost, but in 17 years I never lost a war with a Christmas tree.

When that tree, No. 17, joins its ancestors in Valhalla, the veterans of that decade will say, "You kids have it easy these days. Let me tell you about a REAL Christmas war."

My bouts with Christmas trees are remembered well in this house. For instance, I put up No. 17 the other day and one of the fire truck veterans, now as tall as I, announced, "It's a tribute to man's ingenuity." Another big-shot senior in high school, who has helped make a hero out of more than one tree in this house, looked at it and shouted, "Another triumph for technology".

But now, like the very early days before the action got heavy, there's only the initial skirmish, and the tree stays where I put it.

Listen to me and you wouldn't believe it, I suppose, but I miss those fighting trees. As a matter of fact, I never met a Christmas tree I didn't like.

Christmas Eve would wear Ma and me out, wear us right out, even if the tree behaved in that dizzy, whirling, happy decade.

But there was never a Christmas Eve, including this one, when we didn't sit waiting for the sun with a cup of coffee, our work done, gazing at the tree and thinking, "Christmas tree, Oh, Christmas tree, how lovely are thy branches."

# Nineteen Seventy-Six

*This one, the signature column of this collection, was fun to write, and oh, so true.*

# Thanks, Santa, But Who's Gonna Put it Together?

**December 25, 1976**

This is the letter I left for Santa Claus last night:

Dear S.,

Before you go straight to your work, I hope you'll take a minute to sit down, drink this glass of milk, have a cookie or two, and read this message. It is more or less urgent.

Look, I know you mean well, but I'm getting up there, you know, and I can't handle too many more assignments like the one you gave me this year.

I know you're a right jolly old elf, but I also think I know how you stay jolly.

It seems to be standard procedure for you to send things like that bike (over there by the tree) on ahead for people to assemble. Why is it you and your staff (I have been led to believe they are all capable, industrious elves) can not put things together before delivery? If that is not possible, why do you not screen the people you select for this task?

Oh, I don't mean to be harsh, or even critical. I just want to make you aware of a couple of things.

That bike took me many man-hours to put together. And look at it. The kid will say, "Hooray, I got a bike," and then he'll try to ride the blasted thing and the wheel will rub, the saddle will come loose, the chain will flop off, and other untoward things will happen. He'll blame you, which isn't fair, and I'll have to try to rectify all the troubles, which will be difficult because all the nuts are rounded off.

Point is, S., you shouldn't ask a guy who has trouble with paper clips to assemble a bicycle. It's not fair to either of us.

And while I'm on it, what ever happened to games? Where are the checkers, jacks, darts, Monopoly, and pin-the-tail on one animal or another? Good old games, you know, where

Games were always a hit.

you rip off the paper and open the box and there's your game. Nothing to assemble, no moving parts, no problems.

You remember "Put Out Your Hand," the game you brought us a couple of years ago?  I worked through dinner to assemble it — an absolutely incredible contraption of cardboard and plastic, elastic band and tiny springs.  And a list of instructions as tall as a good-sized sleigh.  Listen, be reasonable, will you?

And what about the firetruck.  I don't mean to rake up old complaints, but that firetruck just about ruined me.  Did you know that?  Did you know I stuck a screwdriver in my palm and had to work one-handed after that?  I got it together, and it worked, one-handed.  But what of a man's health?  Is it fair to expose him to such hazards?

I think not, S., I think not.

The metal doll house that came in a flat box bears mentioning, while I'm carping.  Metal tabs, it had, that you put through slots, and bent over.  Slot B did not always line up with Tab B.  And the tabs snapped off so easily and ... well, by the time I got through, it looked more like a factory warehouse than a doll house.

That's really all I have to say and I'm glad I got it off my chest. Whatever you do, don't get me wrong. You're OK in my book, S. It's just that a guy is better off to get things in the open rather than to keep his mouth shut and have them eat away at him. That's my philosophy, anyway.

I do want to say thanks for the good job you've done for us on this Super Bowl of holidays in the past. The gifts are always great, but I've never failed to notice, every December 25, that you also bring something better. Oh, I guess I can't put my finger on it.

Hope, maybe? Warmth? Beauty? You know, the stuff poets sing about. Things you don't have to put together. Keep up the good work.

Best Regards,

C

P.S. If that milk idea doesn't grab you, reach down and to your right. How's that, eh? Go ahead. It's cold out there, and who's gonna know?

 Nineteen Seventy-Seven

*The aura which always descended upon us as Christmas approached made Ethel and me appreciate what we had. Our friends didn't know another family with 10 children. Nor did we. But it wasn't the double numbers that made us feel special, it was the fact that they all seemed to be heading in the right direction. They were good citizens and each others' best friends. We were proud.*

*We worked very hard and, pardon me if I seem to crow, we were a terrific team. Up to this point, we had weathered all crises, managed to find humor in most situations, and, while we had hard days, we never had bad days. I attempted to express what I will always consider to be a unique partnership, and the importance of this splendid holiday, in my 1977 column.*

During a quick visit to the *Courant* office in 1971, a staff photographer got us all in this pose. Linda and Sheila are in the back with Dad. Kathy and Owen in the front, and in the middle row, Sharon, Patricia, Maureen, Steven and Kevin. Dan, the baby, had to stay home with his mother.

# Oasis

**December 25, 1977**

The man and the woman were walking through the winter and stopping at each oasis. They walked rapidly and easily because they were young. The snow was deep in places and the wind was strong and cold, but they were warm because they were together.

The road was ill-lighted in some spots but brilliantly lighted in others. When the light was very dim and the snow was deepest they held tightly to each other, and if one stumbled the other was there to say, "Here we go. No problem. We're all right."

The road stretched ahead. The man and the woman knew they must eventually cover it all, but they kept their eyes on the next bright light and so did not concern themselves with the far end of the winter road.

They came to a Christmas oasis and stopped to warm themselves and forget the road. The children were there. Two of the boys were pounding fists into new baseball gloves, fresh from the box. The ponderously adorned tree did not appear to be squarely placed, though the man knew he had anchored it securely. But it would be all right.

In the noise and confusion and laughter, the boys slipped away with their gloves and found a baseball and threw it back and forth in the kitchen. The ball hit the overhead light and smashed the bulb.

The man and the woman rushed to the kitchen. The man flared up, but mellowed quickly because the woman touched his arm and smiled and said "Now, it's Christmas." And the man smiled too.

At night the coffee boiled and had a heady, invigorating smell. The house was in sorry disarray, but incredibly comfortable. The man and the woman made happy small talk about the day, and they didn't care that the winter road waited and that they must take it tomorrow. They would go together.

They went the next day, with Christmas still strong in their heads and hearts and with a spring in their steps. They traveled far, through many places where the light was dim and the wind was harsh and the snow drifted across their special byway. But they held to each other and kept their eyes fixed on the next bright light.

When they came to it they stopped. The sounds of Christmas were there. Carols and the yelps of children and soft singing. The buzzing and clicking of new toys. Crackling log-fire sounds. Thank-you sounds and you're-welcome sounds.

The man sat on the floor and tried the balancing block game. The last block would go on and the structure would collapse and the man gave up after an hour because it was impossible. It was. But the little girl with traces of jelly doughnut on her lips and the soft sweetness of Christmas in her eyes parked her new doll carriage and sat down and did the impossible, first try. The woman laughed and the man went to a private, high shelf he knew about and poured himself a few drops of something he called "pretty good stuff."

The man and the woman left the next day and set out along the road toward the next oasis, and, finding it, savored it, and then went on toward the next and then the next and then the next. Each oasis was a shining, shimmering stop, alive with tinsel and laughter and people saying "Good Christmas" to each other and meaning it. Each oasis was a high, crowning relief point on their special byway.

They stored the experience of each oasis within them. When the light was dim and their steps were less than sprightly, they got out their memories and exchanged them like Christmas gifts.

The man and the woman arrived today at another oasis, with the special sounds and smells and tastes and feelings. The boys who smashed the kitchen light way back down the byway will shave before church, and the little girl who did the careless miracle with the blocks will refuse a jelly doughnut and caution her little brother to be careful of the tree.

Someone will say "We're all home. We're all here for Christmas." The coffee will boil in the evening, and the man and the woman will sift out the special memories and pack them on top of the others, making ready for the morning.

Tomorrow they'll be back on the road with its cutting wind and heavy drifts. And though their steps are not as lively and the byway is dim, they will fix their eyes on the brightest light ahead and hold each other for warmth and press on to the next bright oasis.

# Nineteen Seventy-Nine

*Linda was attending the University of Connecticut, Sheila had chosen St. Joseph's College in West Hartford, and Owen was enrolled at the University of Oklahoma. All would be home for Christmas. The 1979 column was a summing up.*

Maureen mellows out in her new coat while Dad digs, 1987.

# And Why Not?

**December 25, 1979**

**I** like Christmas, Mister.

I like the airport and the hugging that comes with each deplaning, holiday hugging, homecoming hugging. Hugging was invented at airports by people coming home.

I like my house to be a hotel, as it used to be and as it is today and as it will always be in late December and into January. I like not knowing who will next walk in the door to shake hands and say, "Good to see you again."

I like a smash of the good stuff with droppers-in.

I like never having my own car around when I need it and having to stand in line to make a call on my own telephone.

I like "A Christmas Carol," with Ed Begley.

I like music, laughter, arguments in voices I haven't heard for too long.

I like a Christmas tree, heavy with gaudy trimmings, that can take a clean hit in the open field of the living room and still keep its feet.

I like bulbs that flicker out, always in the very back and always most difficult to reach.

I like doughnuts at 6 o'clock, lasagna at 1, and a sandwich at 7.

I like being tired all day, and making it through on that reservoir of adrenalin the spirit supplies.

I like passing out a sea of gifts to 11 people (and myself) seated in a very large room that isn't half large enough.

I like "The Little Drummer Boy."

I like boiling coffee for just Ma and me to drink deep in the night when the work is done.  We used to have our coffee when everybody was in bed.  Now, when we have it, nobody's in yet.

I like little presents in enormous packages.

I like Nerf basketball games, two-on-two in the sunroom, that rattle the windows.

I like smiling at things that, 364 days of the year, would make me blow up like a land mine.

I like shirts that don't fit, cars that don't start, dogs that don't stop barking.

I like the expression "the goose hangs high."

I like the memories of sugarplum Christmases, and the making of more; the dense atmosphere of mellow warmth; arms around my neck like a wreath; mixed nuts in a bowl and Christmas cookies on a plate; great fluttering blankets of discarded wrapping paper; people who care and people who care for me.

I like knowing that nobody has really been away, or will ever really be away. I like that best.

I like Christmas, Mister.

# Nineteen Eighty

*This was the year of our 25th wedding anniversary, and what a year it was! The children organized a surprise party for us and carried it off beautifully. We were lured to a church hall on a Saturday. When we entered, every-one we loved was in the room. There were 75 friends and relatives there. We renewed our marriage vows and danced to the music of a live band. Borrowing money from each other, all the children had come home.*

*Ethel and I agreed it was the greatest day of our lives. That Christmas my column was nothing but an open love letter to her. I feel the same way about her today.*

Cutting the cake at our surprise 25th anniversary party in May, 1980.

# She'll Do It All, Christmas Will Be Perfect Again

**December 25, 1980**

The one woman in the life of this sportwriter is many women. I have practical gifts for all of them this Christmas, because they have been with me 25 years.

How's this? They will get a day off. I will not have them lift a finger. They will sit today, all day. I'll do it all. Every bit of it.

*And I will pay them a day's pay, at the going rate.*

A practical gift, eh? And a Christmas bonus besides.

The cleaning lady is only 5-1, 120 pounds, with salt and pepper hair that smells like, I don't know, lilacs maybe, and a smile like a Christmas star. (I've got a thing going with her ... don't tell the cook.) I've got a nice day planned for her. I'll be alert today. I'll beat her to the vacuum cleaner when the tinsel scatters. I'll carry a damp sponge with me at all times, and when a drink goes over, I'll pounce on it. "Sit still," I'll say. I'll shout it if I have to. I'll just order her to enjoy her leisure. I'll insist on it. She won't have to budge from her chair, because I'll find a big box and pick up and dispose of every scrap of discarded wrapping paper. And tonight, before she can make a move for it, I'll grab the broom and sweep the rug near the front door.

I have a nice Christmas planned for the cook (see description of cleaning lady.) She sits down today. That's all. No standing at the stove with a serving spoon while all of us file by to get our traditional lasagna, which she prepared last night. I do the serving today. She doesn't even make coffee. I do that. I make the sandwiches at supper time. She sits. "Be lazy, one time," I'll say. And I'll bring her a piece of Christmas cake and coffee and wait on her. This is my practical gift to the cook.

My secretary (see description of cook) will be in, and I've got the same nice surprise for her. I will hide every ball-point pen, every ledger, every bankbook and checkbook. I will permit her to do nothing but sit on the couch with the others. I will get the peanut butter jar she uses as her bookkeeping file, and stuff it with price tags and receipts. I will record the sweaters that don't fit, all the things that must be exchanged. "Don't worry," I'll say. "I have it down here in the book. Take it easy today. This is your day to sit."

The dishwasher (see description of secretary) will touch neither sponge nor rag nor soapy water this day. I swear it. She will scrub no pans, rinse no endless army of glasses. I will man the sink and insist that she not interfere. "Today," I'll say, and it will be a command, "is your day to sit. Go now and be slothful." I'll be firm.

The nurse (see description of dishwasher) will be amazed at my facility for patching and dispensing. If there is a sliver to be removed, I'll be first with the needle. I know where the aspirin is hidden. I can bandage a cut. I can test for a fever with a palm to the forehead. I've watched her. I know all the tricks, all the cures. "I'll handle it," I'll say, and order her to join the others just relaxing on Christmas Day. My gift.

I'll ... I'll...

I'll do nothing. Nothing. The women in my life simply won't allow it.

In the consecrating confusion of a house that we filled and is full once again — Christmas full — the cleaning lady will smile her bright-star smile, and kid me for my foolishness and say, "I know you're trying to help, but it's easier if I do it. Want to help me? Go sit down. That will help." And the cook will say, "We have to move it along, so just let me ... ." And the secretary will say, "I know exactly what I need. Thanks, but ... ." And the dishwasher will say, "There's a trick to a sticky pan like this." And the nurse will simply take over if there is a crisis, before I have a chance to react.

It's clear I must make do with a gift that is purchased, wrapped and tagged, like always; a gift that will be the wrong size and color and will not be practical at all.

The one woman in my life will open it and hold it up for her 10 children to see and say, "Oh, it's lovely," just as if it really were, and just as she has done on 24 previous Christmases.

My gifts from her will be exactly the right things. Perfect.

In the thundering silence of the soft Christmas evening we will sit alone. There will be coffee, few words, and a look. A look. Our eyes will meet for one swift moment and the look in mine will tell her "Thanks for 25 years of always giving the right gifts, the perfect gifts." And the look in hers will be another perfect gift to me.

Her head will nod. I'll notice the salt has won its war with the pepper, making her more beautiful, and the scent of lilacs will enchant me.

She will doze. Christmas is a busy day for the one incredible woman in my life.

# Nineteen Eighty-One

*Looking back on past Christmases and relishing this one, when all of us would gather again in this great house to celebrate the moment and each other.*

Dan and his sister Linda.

Ethel referred to her
daughters as the big
girls, medium girls, and
little girls. These are
the big, Linda and Sheila,
and the mediums, Kathy and
Sharon. The kids usually
enjoyed having their
pictures taken, but on this
day Kathy had a problem
with it.

Bathtime for, left
to right, Steve,
Sharon, Kevin,
and Kathy.
Way back when.

# When Calm Could Rattle the Rafters

**December 25, 1981**

All is calm and all is bright, and the calm in my house represents change. For a decade in the old days there would be an added starter or two around the tree just about every Christmas morning. Bright was always there, but calm meant "nobody's bleeding and there are no bones broken." Today, all is calm, all is bright. Period.

Funny what a man remembers from ever-bright Christmastimes in that era when the definition of calm was "not yet completely out of control."

"Hello. Hello, Dad? Hi. Guess what? The tree fell down."

"Where is your mother?"

"She's trying to get Steven out from under the tree."

"Are there any injuries?"

"Yes, the tree is hurt bad."

"How did it fall."

"It just fell."

"I see. The tree was standing firm this morning. It was fine. Am I to understand that it just fainted?"

"I guess so. Anyway, can you come home early? Mom wants you to."

"Oh-oh. What is that sticking out of the cake?"

"It's my new football. I'm sorry."

"I thought I told you guys not play catch in the house."

"We weren't. It just ... well, it slipped."

"It slipped? It slipped 10 feet and ruined your mother's special three-layer cherry Christmas cake that took her three days to build?"

"I'm sorry. Can you wash it for us?"

"What's the matter? No crying on Christmas, remember?"

"The boys broke my doll carriage in the hall. Look, the wheel's off."

"How'd it happen?"

"They were wrestling. They wouldn't get out of the way."

"And?"

"And I ran over them."

"I can't get this @$%!&* thing together."

"No swearing, please. Christmas. Besides, you'll wake the kids."

"But it says Tab C into Slot C, and there is no Slot C."

"Let's see. Ah, here we are, it goes on the other side."

"No, it can't."

"Sure. Watch. There. Now the roof will fit perfectly on those two ridges if you can straighten out where you bent it."

"I'll be darned. Hey, you do this. I'll wrap."

"Open my present next."

"All right. Hey, wow. Mittens, right? You knit these for me? These are great. I like this color, too. I love pink."

"Do they fit?"

"A little tight, but don't worry, they're supposed to be tight at first. Umm ... there's no ... ummm ... no thumbs in these mittens."

"I don't know how to make thumbs."

"Go back upstairs. It's not time yet."

"I heard Santa Claus talking."

"You couldn't have. He hasn't been here yet. It's only 11 o'clock. He won't come until you're asleep."

"Does he fill the stockings first or put the presents under?"

"His routine varies. Please go to bed."

"Will you see him?"

"Yes."

"Can I sleep in your bed?"

"No. Oh-oh, who's that?"

"It's me. I heard Santa Claus talking ..."

"That is jelly up there, isn't it? That big red splotch?"

"Never mind."

"Ummm, I don't mind. I mean, I really don't because it's Christmas, but I'm curious. How did that big blotch of red jelly get on the kitchen ceiling that you had me rush to paint a nice white-white for the holidays."

"The boys said they had their new gloves and weren't supposed to use a baseball in the house, and so they began catching with ... er ... a jelly doughnut. It didn't hurt anything. They were just lobbing underhand, until ... they started throwing popups."

"I see. Wonder what the gloves look like?"

"Watch where you're walking till I get a sponge."

"Don't tell me they were throwing grounders, too."

And here are a few lines of 1981 Christmas dialogue. "Hey, anybody home?"

"Yipes, it's her.  The last one's in."
"Everybody here?"
"Now, yes.  At last."
"Well, Merry Christmas, then."

All is calm, comparatively speaking, and all is very, very bright.

# Nineteen Eighty-Two

*For the first time, one of us would be missing at Christmas. Owen's schedule in Oklahoma would keep him there. We were comforted by the fact that he would spend the holiday with his fianceé, Lori Markle, and her parents. But there would be a void on Woodbine Street. I tried to find the best way to express what it meant to have one empty chair.*

Linda, Sheila, and Owen wait for Santa. About 14 years
later Owen, a student at the University of Oklahoma,
would be the first to miss a Christmas on Woodbine Street;
but he was there in spirit.

# This Classic Is Different: It's 3-on-2

**December 25, 1982**

There has never been a substitute in the Four Brothers Football Classic (FBFC), because there never before has been an absent player.

You can understand my misgivings, this disquieting feeling. Pressure? Yes. One game that lacks the customary competitive fire could make the FBFC nothing more than a memory, and change the flavor and order of Christmas around here.

Don't worry about it. I am the substitute, and I believe I am ready. I am not blowing smoke, or talking big. I have reason, at last, to believe Dan and I can win this thing. Well, I do. My attitude has changed. I made a phone call.

We will have them outnumbered.

There are four players in the classic. Half of them, usually, come in from the West. They come home to celebrate Christmas and to play in the FBFC.

The game always has been played on Christmas night. A new foam rubber football is introduced. Street lights offer sufficient illumination. The field is the blacktop street, usually covered with ice and snow. The goal lines are two telephone poles. The final score is usually 72-66.

I have seen the classic played in roaring snowstorms and in hail, and on nights that were warm and pleasant for December. It is played without fail, no matter what.

You must understand the importance placed upon it. The oldest brother, Owen, and the youngest, Dan, a high school freshman, go up against Steve and Kevin. The sides have never changed (until today), and the winners are obnoxiously arrogant for a whole year. The suffering losers have no chance for redemptive action for 365 days.

We learned weeks ago that Owen, a working stiff in the West, could not make Christmas in Connecticut. This is a first. "But I'll be there," he said, "like the song says, in my dreams."

Of course. But what of the classic?

"Looks like it's up to you, Paw."

Just like that, eh? Up to me.

Oh, it was disquieting. There was a time … but he was remembering legs that could churn and a limber arm. He was remembering a lesser, lighter quarterback. He was remembering the first passer who ever instructed him "go to the corner of the garage and cut for the curb." He was remembering when I was the taller one, the more mobile one, the one who could heave that thing from pole to pole and road to river. He was remembering pre-FBFC days.

Up to me.

The anxiety would not lift. I would be a substitute in the classic, the first substitute ever. Do you understand pressure? This game can't be played with less than four, four who can catch and throw and take a check into a snowbank or a hedge. Four who can run. Four brothers. I saw myself as I was 10 years ago, and gave myself a pep talk. "The legs can still churn; the arm is fine; you have not grown *that* fat." And the voice of truth came back. "They can? It is? You haven't?"

Up to me.

Yesterday, I made the call. "I need advice," I said. "I need a game plan. I'm a substitute, and I need help."

A voice from the West gave me pointers.

"All right, look. You rush. Let Dan handle the pass defense. Defense still wins football games, even in the classic.

"Offense. If Kevin's playing back, take him deep. Use buttonhooks and cuts on Steve. He's faster." And other things I can't yet reveal, a guaranteed trick play among them.

"Thanks."

Pause.

"Get the tree up, all right?" Laughter from the West.

"Yeah. Like always. Wrestling a room full of porcupines. But it's up ... listen ... well, we'll be thinking about you. Hear me?"

"Same here." said a huskier voice from the West, "But the thing with Christmas, Paw, I know, is you can be there without being there. Know what I'm saying? A guy can be there. So look for me in my old place."

"Yeah ... you look for us in your new one."

Younger, I said goodbye, and my legs felt strong. I flexed my throwing arm. Loose. Limber. I found a mirror and looked and saw the blurred image of an athlete.

The Four Brothers Football Classic goes tonight and the pressure is off. Our opponents are tough, but I doubt they can handle the three of us.

 # Nineteen Eighty-Three

*The little boy described in the following column is modeled after one who lived at the far end of Woodbine Street with his mother. The family had little. Mike (not his real name) enjoyed stopping at our yard. He took to Ethel, who usually had a cookie at the ready. He moved away after less than a year. We never knew where he went and never heard from him again.*

A familiar sight.
Feeding Sheila, 1958.

Ethel and her seven
children in the summer
of 1965.  Steve is
seated in the driveway.
The others,
left to right,
Sharon, Kevin, Owen,
Kathy, Sheila, Linda.

# Christmas Is a Time for Giving

**December 25, 1983**

Mike hurried home, clutching the gift his third grade teacher had helped him make for his mother. It was a picture of a football player, running. He had drawn it and painted it and placed it in a frame. She had wrapped it for him.

His mother would like the picture, but it troubled him that this was the only gift he could give. He wished he had money and more gifts to give, and more people to give them to, a brother or sister, at least. He did not even think of a father.

He would receive presents the following morning, Christmas. Last year, his mother watched him unwrap his gifts, and shared his excitement. The football had been best, though he knew probably least expensive. It was a white plastic thing, not near to regulation, but it was a wondrous thing to hold in his hands, and spin in the air.

Mike was proud that the neighborhood guys demanded that his ball be used in the street games every day after school. You couldn't kick the white ball — he wouldn't allow it — but it was perfect for passing. For a boy of 9, he could throw a football well, people said. He liked the running and rough stuff, too, and, if a fight developed, he didn't mind that either.

He stopped, as he had every day for a week, to admire the creche on the Farroughs' wide lawn. He could see the ceramic figures of the Nativity, with the Christ child at its center. The figure in the tilted manger had sad eyes and hands uplifted. The creche was elaborate, and surrounded by a low white picket fence. It was lighted. People going by at night slowed their cars to admire it. Mike knew the Christmas story and was both saddened and uplifted by it.

Mrs. Farrough, afraid that he would disturb something, called out to him to get along, now, he'd looked long enough. The Farroughs were not friendly to Mike and his mother. He didn't know why. But they had a nice creche.

He was a thin, serious boy, sometimes given to moods. He looked out for his mother the best he could, but he knew she was lonely sometimes, or sad. She never showed him, but he knew. And she took care of him. When he was sad or sorry for himself, she would hug him and coax him back to good humor, saying, "Don't, now. Are you sick? Are you hungry? Are you alone? Well, then, come on old football player. Think about good luck."

She convinced him. When she wasn't there to help, he would tell himself, "Think about good luck." They were just two, going along, thinking about good luck. They had a warm apartment and enough of the other things.

Mike took a last, long look at the ceramic Christ child, who had no warm apartment, and walked the half block to his house. He climbed to the second floor. His mother was home, he knew, because her waitress apron was folded on a chair, where she always left it. He found her in the small living room, fussing with the tree, an angular women with gray starting in on hair that was the color of the winter sun and red hands that wrought workaday miracles.

He put her gift under the tree and cautioned her not to touch it until the following morning. He tried not to show a sudden pensiveness and failed. She hugged him.

"What? Come on. What?"

"Wisht I had another gift to give somebody."

"Nonsense. This will be our best Christmas. Ham, tomorrow, too. You give enough. Think about the good luck."

"But ... OK."

He got the white football from its special place under the bed in his room and went out. The guys seemed to just materialize in the street. Soon they were playing, but it was Christmas Eve and the game dissolved into talk. They talked about Christmas morning, and what they would find under their trees. Mike offered to bet he'd get new boots and a hat. One friend spoke with confidence about a bike, and another of a special Dallas Cowboys jacket.

And then the others spoke about what they had purchased for other people with money given them for that purpose. "Got my sister a sweater." "Got my father a new pipe." "Got my brother fishin' stuff."

Mike walked alone up the block to the Farroughs' creche and stood looking at the sad eyes of the ceramic Christ child. When he turned away, he was excited and smiling, and, when he got home, his mother was happy to note that his mood had passed. He went to bed early, an excited 9-year-old on Christmas Eve.

He awoke very early, dressed, and fumbled under the bed for the white football. He got a black crayon, snapped on the light, and wrote something on the pebbly plastic surface. He crept silently out of the house.

He was afraid of being caught, but would not turn back. The Farroughs' creche glowed in the dark yard. He walked to the low fence. Not daring to scale it, he leaned over, measuring carefully. He tossed the white football, underhand, with no spin. It landed softly in the straw beside the sad-eyed ceramic Christ child and stayed in the manger. "Nice catch," he whispered, exhilarated with the thrill of giving.

The black crayon message he had scrawled lay partially exposed. It said:

"Good luck. Mike."

# Nineteen Eighty-Four

*We never got a great deal of time alone around Christmas, but when it did happen we mellowed out and did a lot of laughing, remembering what it once had been.*

A snack before bedtime, mid-1960's.

A friend took this photo of, left to right, Kevin, Linda, Kathy, Sheila, and Owen in our living room not long after Christmas, 1962.

# Thinking Back on the Night Before the Night Before

**December 25, 1984**

It was 1963. The phone rang in the office.

"Disaster area," She said.

"Again? Any injuries? Much damage?"

"No injuries."

I drove home and put on my heavy gloves and put the Christmas tree back up. It fell again that night, while I was outside shoveling snow. All by itself, I was told. Just took a dive, smasho, onto the rug. I put it up again. It took patience, which I didn't have, and considerable swearing. I had plenty of that.

"Oh, stop," She said. "It's Christmas." She was always so calm.

I was sweating. I had a twig in my eye, and a tiny, teeny piece of shattered ornament in my finger, having fired my gloves across the room, and tinsel draped in my hair and needle scratches on every exposed inch of my body. From upstairs came the infuriating, muffled laughter of people who wanted desperately to laugh, but wanted just as desperately not to be heard laughing.

I delivered the now-famous "Normal Human Beings" speech for the first time. Over the next 11 years, I would deliver it as many as four times in a Christmas season, to as many as 10 listeners.

The Christmas tree never falls down anymore. Look at this one, filling the same living room corner where 24 predecessors stood. It is very large. Very full. Beautifully shaped. Perfectly trimmed. Majestic, a visitor called it. Not one light bulb unlit. Not a trickle of tinsel out of place. It stands there, all proud and untethered, daintily balanced in its three-legged stand.

Majestic, eh? Arrogant, I call it. Disdainful. Haughty, even. Standing there on the very spot where its ancestors fought and died. They thought they were invincible, too. Balancing there, looking pretty, without a care in the world, an unscarred, unscathed, uncaring tree, blissfully ignorant of its history.

"Remember," I said, "no football near the tree, like last year. No rough-housing. No wrestling. No racing on tricycles. No having a catch. No jumping rope. Let's see if we can keep it looking nice. Only three days till Christmas." It was 1966.

That night, I was struggling to put the tree back up, giving the "Normal Human Beings" speech through clenched teeth. "Normal human beings put up their Christmas trees, and when the season is over, they take them down. They don't use them for tackling dummies. This is not a railroad gate that goes up and down when the train goes by. This is not a railroad crossing. It's a fragile Christmas tree. Normal human beings treat Christmas as a non-violent time of year. Peace on Earth, for crying out loud … ."

The little kids had fled. The bigger kids stood around, but at a good distance, showing superhuman self-control by allowing no laughter to escape.

"Will you turn it a little toward the wall, please," said the Calming Voice, "so that we can't see that big, well, broken place."

"The whole thing is a broken place. One big broken place."

"No it isn't. There. Fine. What's wrong with that? Relax. Accidents happen."

These days, if the dog wags his tail and one little ornament falls off, people get excited, and the tree, it seems to me, looks offended, as if saying, "Keep that animal away from me. Don't you know I'm a regal entity, a special thing to be admired and not touched, and certainly not to be wagged at."

Well, pardon my sneer.

1970. Maturing voices of young women from upstairs.

"Daniel backed into it with the fire truck. Maureen was on the back but there were no injuries."

"Oh. What's he saying now?"

"He's on 'railroad gate.'"

"Oh. What's that hammering?"

"He's got some kind of board with a wire on it, and he's nailing it to the divider. And he's got it tied up with some kind of string or wool, too. Mom's arguing, but he's going ahead with it."

"Can you stand it? Can ... you ... stand it?"

"That's it," the Calming voice said in 1973. "Put the hammer away. I won't have my Christmas tree held up with 2-by-4's and chains and ropes anymore."

"But it's only a little strip of wood, fine wire, ..."

"No. Besides, we really don't need to prop it anymore. Really. Do we?" And we didn't.

We sat there on the night before the night before, 1984, examining the tree. We were alone because young adults who have returned for the Christmas moment go out nights, and when they come in, they need not be told to protect the tree.

"It's beautiful. The best we ever had. It's almost ... ."

"Yeah, yeah, majestic. But arrogant, wouldn't you say. I'd like to ... do you mind if ... well, if I knock it down. Just once. Just let me push it over, one time."

She chuckled, understanding. "I was thinking the same thing. I'm tempted to say go ahead. But no. Tell you what, though. I'll listen to a couple of choruses of the 'Normal Human Beings' speech."

"Nope. Last time I gave that speech, you know what I got. Blatant applause."

"I know. I was one of those applauding."

"Can I catch a break around here?"

"How about the time ..."

And we were off on our own little trip in the empty house, laughing so hard with the memories that our eyes watered.    If anybody had been upstairs, they'd have thought we were both crazy.

 Nineteen Eighty-Five

*I believe I could write a book about any one of the Gallant Ten. Although I didn't do a book on Patricia, I felt Christmas of 1985 was a good time to tell her story.*

Patricia, Christmas morning, 1984.

# A Battler Since Birth Brings Joy

**December 25, 1985**

**L**ooking like a little kid, Pat sat in her room, under the January 27, 1985, *Northeast Magazine* picture of Sylvain ("he's beautiful ... bee-yoo-tee-ful") Turgeon, which was taped to her wall. She wore her great winner's smile. She told her parents she had chosen a Big Eight university 1,500 miles away. Against their advice, and the advice of almost all others consulted, she would go there in the fall. And that was that.

"Remember, you didn't stop the others," she said. "I want this. I have to do this. So I've decided to go."

The parents, out of earshot, were apprehensive, but they had always supported her. "Well," they said, rerunning the argument they had used for weeks in a campaign to dissuade her, "she doesn't know what she's getting into. Loneliness and newness and being so far away. She's a scrapper, but ... alone?"

Pat was born, battling, two decades ago, some three weeks before Christmas.

At birth, she had something akin to pneumonia. Touchy thing, the doctors said. But babies like this are resilient. Many are good fighters. Still ... well, be ready.

The father still remembers driving home in the late night, through the city. He stopped on impulse at a church and got out and stood in front of it, craning his neck and sighting up along the tapering steeple, silhouetted against the dark sky. The clouds were racing. He had an ominous feeling.

Pat was home in a week. "She is tough," the doctors said. "That was a pretty good battle she had on her hands to start her life. She's a fighter." She was like an early Christmas present to her relieved parents, four sisters, and three brothers. They showed her all the Christmas things and told her all the Christmas stories. It was very exciting. She slept through most of it; she smiled through the rest. "Will you look at that smile," her father said.

At 3 weeks old, she knew nothing of Christmas. She knew only eating, sleeping, laughing, crying, and fighting. It didn't matter. Those old enough to remember it still agree it was one of the best of many great Christmases.

Pat grew up protecting her territory. Soon she had another sister. Then another brother. She had unbending family support, and she was bright and beautiful and somehow, for every tear, she was able to produce that knockout smile. But why was it? She had more battles to fight then most. Her parents worried.

There was trouble in kindergarten. She was unhappy.

"It's her hearing," a doctor said. "This girl's hearing is impaired by a condition we call ..." and he gave the name. And shortly, it was corrected. Pat's schoolwork improved.

But when that was over, there was something else, and then something else. As she grew, there were disappointments her friends did not have. More than most kids had, it seemed to her and her parents and her brothers and sisters. But she had weapons — the guts of the born battler and The Smile.

Epilepsy hit when she was 15. It did not interfere with school, work, or her social schedule, because it had been identified immediately and just as quickly controlled. But it had its penalties. For example, she could not receive her driver's license until medical proof was given that she had not had a seizure in three years. It was a bitter thing, difficult to smile through, but she did it. She caught rides for three years. She fought the battle. She won.

Sports were important to her. She played hard, and to win. She rooted hard for the Cowboys, Yankees, and Whalers. Sly Turgeon never had a more loyal fan.

Pat worked very hard, saved her money, and went to a community college and got her Associate's Degree. And then she left her apprehensive parents at the airport. There were tears streaming down her cheeks, and theirs, when she boarded the plane, alone, to fly into battles 1,500 miles away. But she was smiling.

She flew home a few days ago to the Christmas meeting place where her brothers and sisters were gradually assembling. She spoke of her adventures, of battles fought and won, in the Middle West. Everyone listened. She was very much the center of attention. Her smile fairly lit up the old house, already bright with Christmas things.

The picture of Sly Turgeon had been removed from her wall in her absence, and the room painted. When she went to her room with her parents, she didn't notice Turgeon was no longer there. "Here's a picture of Jim," she said, producing same.

"Your boyfriend?" the father asked.

"Ummm ... we're just good friends," she said.

When the parents left her, unpacking, the father said, "Can you believe this?" The mother answered, "Well, she's always been a fighter, and this was her toughest, because she did it alone."

"You know what? We were dumb to doubt her. Think about it. Did she ever lose a big one?"

"No."

That night, late, the father went to the church he had visited the night she was born. It was the same type of grim, blustery night he remembered from two decades before. He stood, craning his neck and measuring the steeple against the dark sky. The clouds were racing. He had a feeling of triumph.

He went home then, knowing this was more than another great Christmas. It was a victory party.

# Nineteen Eighty-Six

*The portrait, still hanging in the very spot where I mounted it, will be 20 years old on Christmas Day, 1995.*

A proof of the portrait. Dan, Owen, and Kevin are seated. Sheila, Sharon, Linda, Patricia, Steve, Maureen, and Kathy stand in the back.

# The Gift: Picture Perfect

**December 25, 1986**

The portrait is 11 years old. Exactly 11 years ago to the day, I hung it on the living-room wall. It was not one of those jobs you put off until tomorrow.

I'm not much around the house (all right, superhumanly inept, if only an exact definition will do), but that morning I was transformed. I assembled the frame, a task more difficult than it sounds. I put it together calmly, working in the very eye of the Christmas morning hurricane. I drove a nail without hitting one of my 10 thumbs in a precisely measured spot. I hung the portrait, which was then straightened, adjusted again, and then pronounced officially hung.

We all stood there and admired it, and have been admiring it ever since. It smiles across from the living-room wall, centered above the couch.

That morning the living room was, of course, crowded. There are never enough chairs. Half of us sit on the floor.  When the kids were little, I was the big shot who bestowed the gifts with a majestic flourish.  By 1975 I had been demoted, sort of, to the guy who passes out the presents.  A servant.  The 10 of them, aged 8 to 18, lashed me with a cold-blooded ridicule because I wasn't going fast enough, or because the tree was being held erect and stable by a 2-inch-wide board ("What are you doing, building a bridge?" some smart-mouth asked) nailed with train-wreck subtlety to a room divider, or something else.  No mercy, even on Christmas morning.

There was, as always, uninterrupted laughter and no intramural conflict.  Cameras snapped and flashed.  People kidded people.  Christmas, see?

The ritual of opening the gifts one at a time and then making the loop again and again finally ended.  The littlest brother had gifts left and got to rip them open pell-mell, and one of his sisters helped him stack them.

That part ended.

Then the boys brought chairs from the kitchen and we were ordered to sit in them, side by side, like a couple of hockey players in the penalty box or two contestants in a game we used to play called "Witch and Warlock."  I remember actually being nervous and thinking how odd it seemed to be nervous in my house on Christmas morning.  There was a sudden electric feeling in the room and it wasn't because I had the rigged the lights up wrong, although I had.

We were handed two packages and ordered to open the large, flat one first — together. The room grew silent except for the crinkling of Christmas paper.

The scene returns, vividly. We had opened the portrait back side up, so that we had to turn it over.

And when we did ... we sat there in our kitchen chairs with our backs straight, holding our portrait in front of us. And we couldn't do anything but gulp, or say anything that made sense. We couldn't see very well for a while there.

I cannot adequately detail that matchless moment, but it was one that echoes warmly every Christmas.

In the second box was the frame. While everyone got up and began to try things on, while everyone was moving around and the joking and wisecracking had begun, while relatives began to arrive and the general confusion and noise level picked up, I worked on the frame — honest, it was more complicated than it sounds — and got it together. And the portrait was hung in the spot where it has remained to this moment.

Later, we asked, "How did you guys do this without us knowing? How?"

They said "We set it up at the studio for a time when Mom was getting her hair done and Dad was working."

And they assembled in the studio, some taking time off from work, and some walking over from school, the big ones transporting the little ones, and somehow everybody made it to the right place at the right time.

Not every one of the young people smiling out from the portrait is in this living room this year. Two will spend Christmas elsewhere. This is 1986, 11 years later, after all, and the world is a very large place.

But the gift, exactingly planned and purchased with paper-route money, odd-jobs money, baby-sitting money, store-clerking money, and even piggy-bank money by young people who were saving for such things as college, and whose budgets were tight, hangs bright and handsome, lighting up the living room this Christmas Day and every day.

I will pay intense attention to it for a special moment this morning and experience certain warm echoes, and know again that even lacking 100-percent attendance we are all together today and forever.

# Nineteen Eighty-Seven

*Ethel was not herself. While she denied there was anything seriously wrong, even she admitted her energy was waning daily. But she delighted in her two grandsons, Sam, son of Linda and Doug Chamberlain in Manchester, New Hampshire, and Owen IV, son of Owen and Lori in Oklahoma City, Oklahoma.*

The summer of 1987, at my 35th THS class reunion.

*While we were all concerned about her as Christmas came and went, we did not guess that this would be her last.*

*The 1987* Courant *column was a letter to Sam and Owen IV, though they would not be with us, welcoming them to a Canfield Christmas.*

Christmas 1986. Something we had just unwrapped was very funny. That's Sharon in the background laughing with us.

# Greetings, Wish You Were Here

**December 25, 1987**

**D**ear Sam and Owen,

We know that you, Sam, up there in New Hampshire and you, Owen, out there in Oklahoma, can't make it here today because of the alternate Christmas rule. You have commitments to spend your first Christmases with your other grandparents. The alternate Christmas rule has been in effect for some five or six years now. It was enacted well before your times.

We're not hollering, because it's a good rule, a fair rule, and we'll abide by it cheerfully.

We wish you could be everywhere at once, but I was thinking, since the sum total of your ages is only 83 days, perhaps it is a good break that you will have a full year to prepare before your introduction to Christmas Day on Woodbine Street. The day is traditionally, well, active in this house.

By Christmas 1988, both of you will have had the chance to see a little of what the world is all about; get the lay of the land — the flatlands of the Great Southwest and the hills of New England — so to speak. And by then you will have met each other and had the chance to exchange ideas and points of view and information about such subjects as Oklahoma football, New Hampshire skiing, and, naturally, the best of all the sports, baseball, which has no specific geographical points of reference and needs none.

Also, you'll both have your sea legs and be able to get around and fend for yourselves. Sure, you guys will be missed this year, but the more I think about it, the better it sounds. All we need is patience, lads, at your end and mine.

We will, of course, have a decent showing on Woodbine Street today. Don't feel like you're leaving us stranded on a lonely island. Your great-grandparents will be here, with six of your aunts and two of your uncles. People — friends, cousins, great aunts and uncles, second cousins twice removed, neighbors, pals, and friends of pals will flow in and out in noisy streams.

And laughter? Ha! Practice your laughing, you guys. While you're practicing catching a ball with your fathers in the next 12 months — yes, I expect you to do this, too — practice your laughing, because next year you're going to have to do a lot of it just to stay even with everybody else.

Your parents can tell you stories about their Woodbine Street Christmases. Sam, ask your mother about the Rocking Horse Christmas, and about being pitched headlong into a pile of Christmas cookies and decorated pastry. Owen, your father can describe the trauma and drama of the Fire Truck Christmas. The fully decorated tree crashed on that memorable morning ... I mean it just went off like a wagonload of light bulbs, amidst a tangle of arms and legs and tinsel. I'm sure the circumstances are still vivid in your father's memory, since he was at the wheel of the shiny new vehicle at the time.

As you boys have noticed, we identify our Christmases by key words and phrases, such as Rocking Horse and Fire Truck.

Portrait Christmas was one of the mellowest. Doll House was one of nonstop action, marked by a couple of minor injuries (scraped knee, bruised forehead) and damage (cracked window). Sled-dog Christmas was ... oh, listen, I don't want to talk about that one. Anyway, you get the picture.

Gentlemen, it will be a joy to see you one year hence on this date, when you will be romping around the rug, hauling manfully on low limbs of the tree, bumping your heads, having a catch in the house with your new gloves (you can inform your parents I will see to this personally) and generally making all kinds of delicious mischief.

It will be great.

But this year is a joy, too, boys, though you aren't here, because here on Woodbine Street we have two more to miss. Know what I'm saying? Two more to wish were here. Two more to think about when the door closes behind the last guest. Two more. Sam and Owen.

Late tonight in the quiet I'll sit in this room beside the tree and contemplate a recurring miracle that has accompanied every Woodbine Street Christmas. It is an inner miracle of feeling and emotion, and, frankly, I am awed by it. I feel it every day, but the Christmas aura makes it shine like the Star of Bethlehem. It is this: Though we Woodbine Streeters are far-flung around the globe this day, none of us is ever really alone. By ourselves, perhaps; maybe even lonely. But together. Today, tomorrow, forever.

> Merry Christmas, lads,
> Grandpa

# Nineteen Eighty-Eight

*Ethel left us on August 4, 1988. After she died, I traveled to Lac St. Denis, and found the places we had been on the day and evening we met. I had not been back since that night in the fall of 1953. I wanted at least to sketch her story and that of our lives and Christmases together. Christmas Day of 1988 was the right time, and the* Courant, *"my" paper, where so many Christmas columns had appeared, was the right place.*

Ethel in her favorite platform rocker, with Owen in the background. He was master of ceremonies at the 25th anniversary party. When his mother died, he delivered a stirring eulogy to a crowded church.

# Of Christmases Past and Present, and a Girl Named Ethel Riley

**December 25, 1988**

Ethel Riley and other English orphan kids sailed out of Liverpool aboard a vessel called the *Dutchess of Bedford* in the spring of 1940. Arriving safely in Montreal, the party entrained for Victoria, British Columbia.

Ethel was 7 years old and, though tiny, she had been a hardy sailor. Much later in life she remembered enjoying the adventure.

Her first North American Christmas, and the next eight, would be spent at Fairbridge Farm School near Victoria.

The little English girl had a personality that was uplifting. The first years of her life in England had been anything but easy. At age 4, she had found herself in an orphanage in Birmingham. When Nazi bombers began leveling that city, the youngsters were whisked away to live in a medieval castle. She would remember it as great fun.

But cheerfulness and perseverance came naturally to Ethel Riley. In the few pictures taken of her in the

Fairbridge years, she was always smiling. She was small, with flowing dark hair that had a reddish tint. Her attractive glasses seemed to enlarge deep blue eyes in which shone resoluteness and joy of life.

At Fairbridge, finally, there was permanence. The kids did their chores, attended school, and learned to take care of themselves and each other.

They each received a penny a week. Ethel and some of her friends used to save for 15 weeks, and then, on a Saturday, walk to the movies.

"What did you get for Christmas when you lived there?" her children would ask, 30 years and more later.

"Oh, things," she answered.

"Well, what?"

"Oranges and nuts and things."

"Really? Oranges? That doesn't seem like very much."

"We were together at least. All in the same boat. We had each other. We were warm. It was fine."

On a cold November evening in 1953, in a place called Lac St. Denis, 50 miles northwest of Montreal,

Leading Air Woman Ethel Riley, Royal Canadian Air Force, met a guy. He was an airman third class in the U.S. Air Force. They were both 19 years old. He thought he was "some punkins," liked to show off, and had a wise crack on his lips all the time. But for reasons he would never be able to figure out, she seemed to like him. She was 5 feet, 1 inch tall. He made jokes about her size, which she found very funny.

She laughed at his dumb jokes through the whole evening, making him feel much taller than his 5 feet, 11½ inches. They danced. They drank Cokes. The place was hot and smoky and loud. They stepped into the cold Quebec night air and walked down a narrow lane. They stood on a tiny bridge and looked at the moon. "Something's happening here," he said, and felt he had said something very corny.

"Yes," she said. "Something is happening."

He shipped out for Korea in January 1954. They wrote letters to each other every day. At Christmas, she sent him a box loaded with so many goodies he figured it must have cost her a month's pay to mail it. But he didn't worry. She was pretty good with a buck.

She received her discharge from the RCAF and a month later, on May 7, 1955, they were married. He drove a black 1941 Plymouth sedan from Torrington, Connecticut, to Alexandria, Louisiana, his last post before discharge. It was a good honeymoon trip.

Christmas was a warm-weather holiday in Bayou country. They celebrated in their tiny apartment. They gave each other what she called "bitty stuff," a couple of inexpensive doodads each, wrapped and placed under a two-foot Christmas tree.

They were parents for the first time in July 1957, a year after returning to Connecticut. Christmas became a bigger thing that year — and bigger the next and every year thereafter. In 1959, Ethel Riley gave birth to a son on Christmas Day. In 1960, on Christmas Eve, she walked three blocks in a heavy snowstorm to go to midnight Mass. He took her to the hospital eight hours later, after the presents had been opened in their house. The next day, December 26, she presented him with twins. Sixteen months later, twins again. They would have 10 children in a 10-year span and astonish the people who knew them.

"Hey, they think we're out to set records," he joked.

"Some of your jokes aren't funny any more," she came back at him. But still they laughed and enjoyed their children and each other. They were great friends, besides being man and wife, father and mother.

Around the family and their circle of friends, it was said of her, "Ten kids? Well, it would have to be Ethel. Nobody else could handle a job like that."

They had a big house that they were able to buy in 1962 because his GI Bill allowed liberal terms. The house always needed work, and visitors claimed they had never seen such a laughing place. That was her doing.

He worked two jobs. Ethel Riley cooked, cleaned, and reared her children to pay attention first to important things, such as responsibility, respect for others, compassion, and appreciation for what was theirs. Perseverance, industry, honesty, and sacrifice she taught by example. She did magic tricks with the money he supplied, gave him his allowance, wrote all the checks, paid all the bills. He was not skilled in home maintenance or money management. He would rather play ball in the street with the kids than paint the house or cut the lawn.

"I have 11 kids, not 10," she would tell their friends. But she indulged him. She doled out his allowance uncompromisingly, despite his pleas for larger sums. "No. If I give you more, you'll spend more," she said. Outwardly, he sulked and obeyed. Inside, this made him smile.

With all she had to do, and never a break, he worried about her. "Aren't you tired?" he asked one day.

"No," she said.

"But I'm afraid you are."

"Naw."

They looked at each other for a moment and then both began to laugh. He said, "We're two damned liars."

"Yes. But we're OK. We'll make it, Bo," she answered, using a pet name they had for each other.

Crises came, some very serious. She was in charge, and none was ever too much for her. "You're unbelievable," he would tell her.

"Well, I think we're a good team," she would answer, making him feel extraordinarily important.

The years went streaming by. The Christmases were landmarks of great noise, a permeating love and joy. Through the 1960's and most of the next decade as well, they were sled-and-doll-house Christmases, with "bitty stuff" for father and mother. And then it turned. In the 1980's, 10 young adults kept their parents opening their packages long after they themselves had finished.

During the Christmas holiday of 1987, Ethel Riley really was tired. She had done her vast Christmas shopping, wrapping, baking, and cooking as always, but it took more out of her than ever. Her store of energy waned and she began dozing off earlier at night in her chair. "Please, see the doctor," he begged. When she agreed without protest, he knew she was ill.

Her children rallied to care for her through her short, heroic fight with a relentless form of cancer. From around the world, country, and state, the 10 returned to the big house, which still needed work but was filled to bursting. The father had known from the beginning that all 10 had in them many of their mother's admirable, sustaining qualities. They remembered responsibility, appreciation for what was theirs, sacrifice and the awesome power of love that she personified.

They ministered to their mother as she grew weaker and weaker before their eyes. Hearts breaking, they drew strength from her heroism while performing heroically themselves. They bathed her, dressed her, brushed her hair, slept on the floor beside her bed, helped transport her (with indescribable gentleness) to hospital treatments and doctor's offices, gave her needles, held her hand, read to her, and laughed with her. Yes, laughed.

She died on August 4. Her children first made sure their father was all right, and then held tight to each other and wept.

We put the Christmas tree up a week ago. The front windows are trimmed with cheerful decorations.

The family has gathered in this wonderful house and will laugh today, though the very act may pierce our hearts. We will laugh because to do otherwise would be to dishonor her beloved memory and that is unthinkable. And to sustain us and get us through the worst times, we will remember her words about her meager Christmases at Fairbridge Farm: "We are together. All in the same boat. We have each other."

She shines today in each of our hearts, and the Christmas spirit she instilled in us still burns as bright as the Star of Bethlehem.

If I could speak to her today I'd say, "We are not just muddling through, dear little Bo. We are carrying on."

**ETHEL**

**She was our Christmas Star**

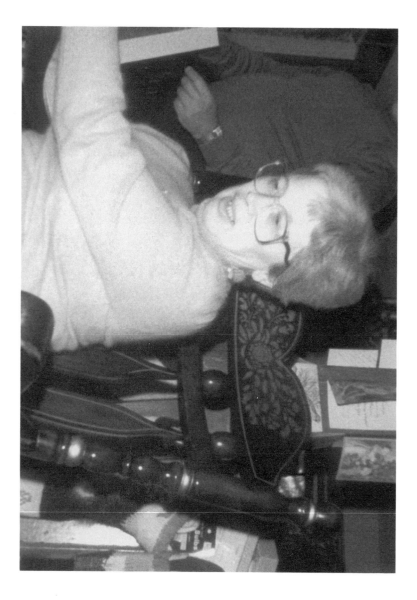

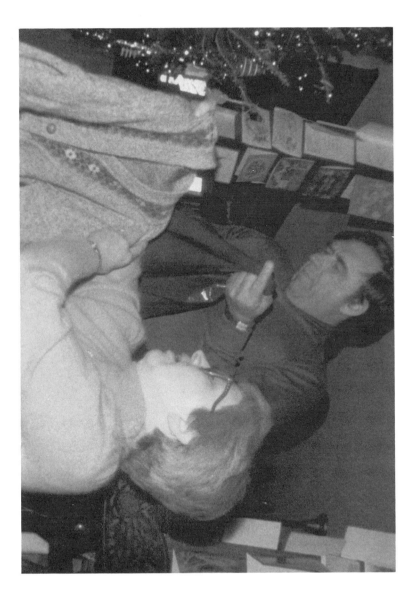

# Nineteen Eighty-Nine

*April came. Twins Kathy and Kevin drove me to the Hartford railroad station where I boarded a train for New York. My ultimate destination was Vancouver Island and Fairbridge Farm in Duncan, British Columbia. I had never visited Vancouver, and I had a strong urge to see the places where Ethel grew up. She had seldom spoken of her childhood, and when she did her answers were sketchy. She offered few details.*

*I had chosen the train because Ethel and I had so often used that mode of transportation before we married, though only once together.*

*Arriving in Seattle, I rented a car and drove to Tssawwassen, just over the Canadian border. A ferryboat called the* Queen of Saanich *brought me to Victoria.   I visited Jack and Joan Burgess and had lunch with Mary in Victoria.   Later I would meet with Rick at little Boundery Bay Airport.   All had fond memories of Ethel.*

*When Ethel "went out" from the farm school to live with Jack and Joan, she finished her high school education at Victoria High and worked in the offices of Royal Jubilee Hospital.   I visited these places before turning north toward Duncan.*

*Ethel's best friend at Fairbridge Farm had been Sylvia Cowens, who had been killed in an automobile accident only a year after she had left the school.   John Cowens, Sylvia's older brother, who had also grown up at Fairbridge, gave me a tour of the grounds.   Many of the houses (they were called "cottages") were still intact, as was the chapel which was being restored.*

*Back in Victoria, I visited the Provincial Archives building and found pictures of Ethel as a child and records kept on her during that time.*

*Emotionally drained, but feeling somehow more complete, I returned home.*

*Later, I learned that she had been taken by her father, Patrick Riley, a coal hewer, to a home for indigent children called Middlemore Home in Birmingham at the age of four.   She was transferred to Shropshire, where she and other children lived briefly in a medieval castle during the war.*

*She was one of the youngest in a party of 30 who shipped out of Liverpool on the Dutchess of Bedford in 1940, landed in Montreal, and then rode the train across Canada, ultimately settling in at Fairbridge Farm.*

*The Burgesses provided a good home for her for about three years, but, until she came to us, she had no real home. From 1955 onward, Ethel showed us all how to live. And then she showed us how to die. Her examples still shine.*

*When Christmas arrived in 1989, I remembered her skill with, and love for, not just her own, but all children.*

Carrying on.

# A Christmas Carol for the Whole Year

**December 25, 1989**

It was summer, a few years ago.

"You've got to like that kid Wilmont," the man said to his wife. "Spunk, you know?"

"Yes," the wife said. "And it's cute the way he looks after his sister."

"He teases her all the time," the man said.

"But he takes care of her," the wife said. "The other day, they were playing on the Monkey Speedway and she scratched her hand. He brought her to the door. The dog was barking, but he kept knocking until I heard and answered and fixed them up with a Band-aid and a cookie."

Wilmont was 8, and his sister Michele was about 5. They lived on the third floor in the house-of-many-colors at the end of the street. They had nothing but big smiles and spunk and what adventures they could find on the brush and tree-covered dike that had been built after the flood of 1955.

The dike, which ran behind the row of houses on the west side of the street, had been a playground for a couple of generations of neighborhood kids. Those who had bikes rode them on the worn path at the top of the dike. Some-one nicknamed it the Monkey Speedway in the long-ago. The name endures.

Occasionally, when the man and his wife were cooking out, Wilmont would materialize, and stand looking down from the dike.

"Want a hot dog, Wilmont?" the woman would offer.

He'd say "OK," and turn and call "come on," and Michelle would then materialize. They liked hot dogs so much they sometimes ate two.

Wilmont hung out around the man's house at the other end of the street frequently. He was always after the man to tighten up loose bolts or fix the chain on his rattletrap bike, or to "borrow" fishing equipment he knew the man kept in his garage. He would stare at the saw and hammer and things hanging in the garage and say, "You've got a bunch of tools." Actually, there were few. The man wasn't handy. But it looked like a bunch to Wilmont.

Wilmont loved baseball. Loved it. "I'm on the Tigers," he told the man, enthusiastically. "Saturday mornings. It's the farm league, 'cause I'm 8."

He loved to sing, too, but he apparently knew only one song, "The Star-Spangled Banner." The man heard him singing it as he rattled by one day and called out. "Hey, Wilmont, c'mere."

"What?"

"Let's hear that again."

"Ohhh, Shea can you see ..."

"No, its 'Oh, say can you see.' Say, not Shea."

"No sir." Wilmont was indignant and impatient with the man's ignorance. "It's Shea. I saw the Mets on TV. I heard this guy sing it. They play at Shea, right? It's Shea. That's why they..."

"Go get your glove," the man said one day. "We'll have a catch."

He stalled and finally said, "I'm getting a new glove Saturday. I lost my other one. Somebody stoled it."

"Wait a minute," the man said. He went in the house and reappeared with a small glove and a big one and a ball. When they were through with their catch, the man said, "Why don't you use that one until you get your new one."

Wilmont said fine, he would borrow it, and went off singing, "Ohhhhh, Shea can you see," carrying the tune very well in his strong small voice and making up the rest of the words.

"That kid is indomitable," the man told his wife, laughing. She agreed.

December came and Christmas time settled sweetly on the street with wreaths on the doors, lights in the windows, and displays on lawns. But there were no lights brightening the house-of-many-colors.

Wilmont came pumping down the snowy street on his rattletrap a few days before Christmas, just adventuring.

He wore a ragged jacket and sneakers. The man leaned on his shovel. "Hey, it's my man Wilmont. Got your Christmas tree up yet?"

"Not yet. I'm going to get us one," he said, and rattled away.

"Poor kid, he looks like a St. Louis newsboy," the man said to his wife. "And no Christmas tree."

"He'll be all right," the wife said. "Like you say, he's got spunk."

The day before Christmas the man, who had the day off from work, noticed that his saw was missing. "Where did I put that thing?" he groused.

And his wife said, "Keep looking, it's got to be around."

That afternoon they took the dog for a walk around the block. As they turned the corner on their street, the wife said, "Look, isn't that Wilmont and Michele?"

Ahead, the two children labored resolutely to drag a ragged, splintery branch of pine along the sidewalk toward the house-of-many-colors. They knew if they followed the trail of pine needles backward it would lead to the Monkey Speedway.

The man said, "He must have borrowed my saw. Damn, it's nothing but a few bare twigs."

"No, it's a Christmas tree. A beautiful one," said the wife who was wise.

Thrilled by what they saw, they drew closer to the trudging children and heard a small, gallant voice singing, "Ohhh, Shea can you see ..."

"He's singing the Star-Spangled Banner," the man whispered.

"No," said the wife. "Don't you know a Christmas carol when you hear one?"

# Nineteen Ninety

*While Christmas had changed dramatically in my house, the memories were still vivid. I did not want to discontinue the Christmas columns. Readers still enjoyed them, and I still got great pleasure from writing them.*

*In 1990, the epistolary style seemed the right way to go.*

Linda and Sheila aboard Plaster Paint.

# The Memory of Ethel Keeps Christmas Alive

**December 25, 1990**

Dear Ethel,

It's Christmas Eve. My 1990 Christmas report deals mostly with the rocking bulls I bought for our grandchildren. I'll get right to it.

I delivered the bulls personally to Oklahoma in November and New Hampshire early this month. In each case, I was able to smuggle these wooden wonders into the house and put them in a foolproof hiding place. No problem.

The guy that handmakes these bulls also does a line of rocking camels, horses, and cows. The bulls, though, jumped out at me when I visited his showroom. No two are painted alike. Both have comical expressions on their faces, which cracked me up, reminding me of Ferdinand, the sissy bull we used to sing about. Remember this?

> "Ferdinand, Ferdinand,
> The bull with the delicate ego,
> Ferdinand, Ferdinand,
> He called everybody *amigo*,
> He learned to tango, and dance the fandango,
> But he never learned to fight."

These oak animals are also pretty mellow, and let me tell you, they are built to last, weighing 60 or 70 pounds apiece. I'm confident they will endure until the cows come home. (A little joke there, girl.) Anyway, we're talking solid here.

I got a discount because I bought two of them. (Just call me Joe Bargain Hunter. In the 2½ years since you went home, I have wrestled the checkbook into submission. Only $16 off last month and that was on the high side. Are you proud, or what?)

The two older grandkids, Sam and Little Owen, will have no problem riding the bulls this Christmas morning, because they are both 3 years old and will be able to scramble aboard and rock all day. Besides, I can tell, and the world will soon learn, that both of these boys are born athletes. Wish I could see their faces when they spot the bulls beside their Christmas trees.

The two little ones, who arrived after you left, and were given your maiden name, Riley, for their middle names, will need help. When Sarah Riley up north and John Riley out west, want to ride, they'll have to be lifted aboard by their parents, or, Lord have mercy, their older brothers. Sarah won't be 2 for a few months and Johnny is just closing in on 1. While both are obviously advanced far beyond their years, they're just too short for bull riding. Not to worry. They'll get bigger.

You know what inspired me to buy one of these things for each household, don't you?

If my math is right, it was exactly 25 years ago that Santa Claus brought Old Plaster Paint to our house. Old Plaster was mounted on a steel-pipe frame and was spring-powered.

He was made of some kind of smooth synthetic material that looked like plaster of Paris and held up beautifully for years. He was handsomely painted too, to look like your classic quarterhorse. But the kids worked him like a freighter's mule.

Poor Old Plaster was hopelessly outnumbered. They used to ride him three at a time at night, and the springs would be stretched to the max in their frame, squealing and squawking like a thousand rusty hinges.

I can see the kids now, clear as pure water, in their pajamas before bed, backing and forthing, three in a line on his back while Old Plaster's springs squeaked and squawked in easy rhythm. He never quit. What a noble animal!

How about the time somebody — was it Sheila? — decided the baby — was it Maureen? — should have a ride. She hopped on and a second conspirator — was it Linda? — hauled the baby out of her crib and handed her up.

Every heart was in the right place  The kids were taught to share.  But it just wasn't a good idea.

Luckily, one of the boys — was it Owen? — was standing by, and when Sheila lost her grip and the baby pitched over Old Paint's head, he was there.  While not able to make the catch, he managed to deflect the airborne baby so that she landed on the enormous Raggedy Ann doll lying on the floor nearby.  Lucky.

The next day, when the emergency had passed and we were alone, did we laugh?  Ha, not much.  Those were the days, eh girl?

So much for Christmas beasts of burden.  As to the rest, for the second straight year, I put the tree up in the sun room.  It's not as big as the ones we used to have, but it looks good with the new wicker furniture, and the lights, seen from the street, tell strangers we still live here and this is our special time.

Have to go.  I'm making something called crunchy drumsticks for the buffet tonight.  I wear your red apron when I cook and make sure I follow the directions.  It gets me by.

Here's tonight's lineup: Sheila and Chris, Kevin, Kathy and Tom, Sharon, Steve and Tammy, Tricia, Maureen and John, Dan and Christine, and me. We'll miss the four in Oklahoma and the four in New Hampshire, but new traditions are being established in those places. Wish I could see the little ones when they spot those Ferdinands, though. At least I know you'll see them because you will be there, dear Ethel, in all three houses.

One more thing, as if you didn't know. Tonight, when all have gone and the singing and carrying-on has stopped, and the trumpets of the angels are playing, I'll sit on the couch and sip my coffee, as the two of us did each Christmas Eve for 33 years after our work was done.

I'll see you there, and I promise I'll not be sad or feel sorry for myself. Rather, my heart will be happy on this, my third Christmas without you, for each one reaffirms more deeply my everlasting love for you. The memory of you is to me that which is Christmas.

Thanks for that.

Owen

# Nineteen Ninety-One

*Another letter to Ethel. I was to host a Christmas Eve party. It eased my nerves to tell her about it.*

Now, what the heck is this? Hope I don't have to assemble it!

# A Tree,
# a Family,
# an Everlasting Gift

**December 25, 1991**

**D**ear Ethel,

It's Christmas Eve. Hope there will be time to finish this Christmas report to you before the kids arrive.

If I'm nervous, well, bear with me, girl. I'm Joe Host tonight and I want things to go well. Frankly, I'm worried about our newest grandbaby, Rachel, remembering what happened in 1962 to Rachel's father, Steve. I'll explain my misgivings in a minute.

I have only this moment finished wrapping. What a mess. You would think after practicing all these years, a man would be able to wrap a Christmas present neatly and without stress or temper. These look like they were done in the dark by a 5-year-old. I'm still all thumbs. Must have used a mile of Scotch tape and an acre of paper.

Once again, I put the tree in this front room, which I now call the Wicker Room. Almost from the day the tree went up, I've been getting sarcastic heat when the kids drop in because this is where all my plants are. When Tricia first saw the room she said, "Ah, Christmas in the tropics." Sharon says the room looks like a hotel lobby. She has taken to calling me "Innkeeper". Cold-blooded children you raised.

Because of all the other greenery, this Christmas tree is smaller than usual — only about 5 feet tall.

I'm into plants these days. I water them every three or four days and they flourish. Fool's luck.

With the big, potted ficus tree, which reaches almost to the ceiling in the middle of the room, the huge hanging spider plant, and that sprawling, leafy thing on the floor in the corner, plus the table, tall lamp, and all the wicker furniture, you can barely move in here. Clumsy people beware.

Just for fun, and because I thought it would look good, you'll notice I hung a few leftover ornaments on the ficus and one on the wicker lamp shade. "The very essence of tackiness," Kathy called it, but I think it looks cool.

I should have anticipated crowded conditions and put the Christmas tree in the large square living room where it always used to be, rather than this long narrow front room. You always said I couldn't plan a walk around the block. Too late now.

This is Rachel's first Christmas. She's too little to know it, but from the moment Tammy and Steve carry her through the front door and into this yuletide jungle she'll be the star.

Our fifth grandchild is just about perfect, as if you didn't know. I realize you had to go home three years ago, but I wish you could have seen her. Prettiest kid in Connecticut. Tammy says she is good-natured and sleeps a lot, just like she's supposed to. She'll probably be a crawler like her dad.

That's what worries me a little. You always said I borrowed trouble, but I can't help remembering the Christmas of '62.

We had Linda, Sheila, Owen, Kevin, Kathy, Steve, and Sharon then. Tricia, Maureen, and Dan had not yet come along, but we were off to a good start. Steve and Sharon were 8 months old.

Remember that Christmas Day? The "aura" was upon us and things were chaotically wonderful. You and I had been up almost all night, wrapping and drinking coffee by the pot. As always, we went to the earliest church service and by 8 o'clock the kids were opening their mountains of presents.

My job was always collecting the discarded wrapping paper in a huge carton. That was part of your system.

About mid-morning, the house was a chamber of noise and wonder and we were both busy playing the games, assembling some things, and repairing others. And suddenly, you said, "Where's Steven?"

We looked around. We looked around some more. Then you said, "All right, everyone look for your brother."

Where could he have crawled to? We searched every room. Had he slithered outside when I opened the door to go out to the car for a moment? No. There were no slither marks in the snow. Down the cellar stairs? No. Upstairs? No.

It got scary for me, but you said, "Don't be silly. He's got to be here."

Then you found him. "Owen, come and look," you called from the parlor. You were laughing your head off.

Steve had pulled the big box of wrapping paper on its side and crawled in. He was sleeping the sleep of the innocent amid the uproar, covered almost completely by scrunched-up wrapping paper.

Talk about peace on earth, eh girl?

Anyway, something like that couldn't happen with Rachel, could it? She's only 2 months. Of course not.

Well, otherwise, I'm all set here, I guess. When we're through with the gift-giving tonight, we'll move out of this greenhouse into the dining room. Everyone is bringing food. Should be a feast.

We'll miss the nine kids, spouses and grandkids who are absent from this celebration, but 12 of us will be here.

I've counted you in that number, dearest girl. Of course you're here. I see you in every one of our children and grandchildren. You are the Christmas star that lights my heart and life every day of the year. Thus will it always be. I thank you for that amazing gift.

Uh-oh, I see headlights. Wish me luck.

Merry Christmas,
Owen

# Nineteen Ninety-Two

*The loneliness that comes at Christmastime to a man who has lost his life partner is sometimes difficult to handle. But if he keeps searching, he can find a way.*

Maureen on Christmas morning, 1992.

Sharon, Sheila, and Dan, 1992.

# The Man Who Found Christmas in a Wooden Box in the Cellar

**December 25, 1992**

The man brought the tree home on the Sunday before Christmas and put it in the four-legged stand. It was barely 6 feet tall, like him, and slim and graceful, unlike him.

In the old days, that tree simply wouldn't do. With ten kids to help with the trimming back then, only a big, wide tree that scraped the 8-foot ceiling would fill the bill.

The aura that had seized him at Christmastime for almost 40 years was not yet upon him. That bothered him. "Where is Christmas?" he asked himself.

This was his fifth Christmas as a widower. He knew a guy who lives by himself doesn't need a big tree. His grown-up kids and friends would be running in and out, but he would spend Christmas Eve with a son and his family and Christmas Day with a daughter and her family.

He got excited when he thought of those gatherings, because kids and grandkids would be all over the place both times. Being a grandfather at Christmas, he thought, is about as important as a man can feel or be on this Earth.

He hauled the huge boxes of decorations out of the attic and lugged them downstairs. Only two sets of lights and a fraction of the ornaments were needed. It didn't take long.

He found the cardboard decorations and pasted them on all the windows. He hung the cheerful Merry Christmas sign across the double doorway. He set up the little cardboard manger scene on the coffee table.

Then he sat in his rocking chair and examined his handiwork and said to the tree, "Well, Slim, you don't make a patch on your ancestors, but you'll do."

Waiting for the aura, he became lost in memories of shimmering Christmases that were deafening, full of happiness, laced with love. He closed his eyes and saw new bats, gloves, dolls, tricycles, toys, books, and games. He saw fluttering blankets of wrapping paper, a fat, unstable Christmas tree fearing for its life, and stars in the eyes of his children. He opened his eyes again.

All 10 were grown and gone. This did not evoke melancholy. Just the opposite. It was now for them to make their own Christmas memories. But he wished the aura would come and wondered why it wouldn't.   "Something's missing," he said.

The man came home from work the next day and said to the tree, "Hello, Slim." He sat again for a few minutes, thinking maybe the aura would descend. He tried to prime the pump, thinking of Rachel and Carolyn, Sam and Sarah, Owen, Johnny and Mary Elizabeth, his grandkids. He concentrated on them, one at a time, and delighted in that.

But when he got up to whip up supper, the aura was still avoiding him. "Maybe I'm too old for it now," he thought sadly. "Maybe things have changed too much."

Tuesday evening, he carried a load of laundry to the cellar and tossed it in the dryer. He had about given up on the Christmas aura. Turning, he saw the toy box.

The wooden toy box, 4 feet long, 2 feet deep, once sat in the playroom, which he had converted into his bedroom when, widowed, he changed the home around. It was loaded with wooden baseball bats, junior models mostly, baseball gloves that time had cracked and dried, balls of various descriptions, jigsaw puzzles with pieces missing, dusty dolls, a little barn with scattered plastic animals, model airplanes with bent wings, and more.

The man stood in the cluttered cellar next to the noisy clothes dryer, looking at the toy box for a moment, and was startled to find the aura closing in until it enveloped him in a velvet fog. He began to laugh and said, "Of course," and ran upstairs. Ran.

He gathered all the Christmas wrapping paper he could find and fished the tape from the kitchen drawer and returned to the toy box. He wrapped it all: the worn-out presents of the past, the discarded treasures, all the memories in the box.

It took him four or five trips up the cellar stairs. He arranged it all under and around the smallish tree. He sat down then, and rocked and sang "Jingle Bells" to himself. Then he said to the tree, "You're all right now, Slim. We're both all right."

# Nineteen Ninety-Three

*It is foolish for one man to live alone in a 10-room house. But around Christmas, the heart overrules the head, no contest.*

Memories like this will make it very difficult to leave this old house. A wedding shower for Steven's fianceé Tammy, Tammy and Ethel sit with Patricia, Maureen, Linda, Kathy, Lori, Sheila, and Sharon. The "kids" gave us the dining room set as a 30th anniversary present.

# Roomfuls of Precious Memories

**December 25, 1993**

The man stopped in about supper time to see the house. He was coming from work, a good-looking young guy in a suit. His name was Mr. Young. He had a good smile and, being younger, he called me "sir."

The big dog, Toby, barked and barked and swished his tail, knocking a couple of ornaments off the little Christmas tree, which was not far from the door.

"Don't worry, he won't bite you," I said.

"I know that," Mr. Young said, "and you know it. But does the dog know it?" He laughed nervously and then said, "So, you're selling." He knew I had been widowed for more than five years.

I said, "Yes. Time to go."

"I'm sorry to come by so close to Christmas," he said.

"No problem."

"Could you show me around a little and tell me about the place? It's big, all right. And sturdy looking." I remembered when it wasn't half big enough and barely sturdy enough.

I said, "Glad to. I'm in a Christmas mood, though, so don't mind me. OK? Good. We're standing in the sun room. Right above this doorway, we used to hang a plastic basketball hoop. Owen, Kevin, Steve, Dan, and I would play two-on-two with a Nerf ball. We did it every Christmas for years. Ethel made us stop the practice after an accident one year. We had to tape the window together. She didn't think it looked very Christmasy, what with visitors dropping in and all."

"Hmmm," Mr. Young said.

We moved to the dining room. "The kids gave us this dining room set after they got older. Before that, for a few years, there was a ping-pong table here. That was a Christmas thing. I put the legs on in the garage and buried the screws too deep. Some of them poked through the top of the table. The kids used to get mad when the ball would hit a screw and take an odd bounce. Linda and Kathy were the best players. Ethel wasn't bad, either. By the way, that's why the rug is worn in these spots. From ping-pong."

Mr. Young said, "Oh."

I showed him the giant portrait of the 10 kids, still hanging where I hung it the Christmas morning they gave it to us in 1974. "They snuck out and got it made and paid for it with baby-sitting money, paper-route money, piggy-bank money, and so on. Greatest present we ever got."

"Wow," said Mr. Young, and he counted the 10 of them and asked me to point out which were the twins.

"Now, in this corner was where the Christmas tree stood every year for 31 years," I said. "We always had a big one, not like that little 4-footer in the other room. In the old days, I usually had to put it up two or three times. Kids get exuberant."

"I know, we've got two," Mr. Young said. He was proud.

I said, "That's a good start. Come upstairs with me and I'll show you the bedrooms and then I'll show you the rest down here."

We mounted the stairs to the silent second floor. "It looks pretty barren now, doesn't it? This was Maureen and Tricia's room," I said. We kept walking. "Linda and Sheila slept in here, and ... follow me, Kathy and Sharon were in this room. And the four boys slept in here, up over the sun room. Look out this window. See that ledge? Kevin climbed out there one summer day when he had been sent to his room. His friend Lee came by and started throwing pine cones up to him. He fell. Luckily, I had just dug up the lawn to plant a new one. He didn't get hurt. But he had to go around and walk in the back door right past his mother. Ethel said he was as white as a sheet."

Downstairs again, we stood in the kitchen. "Mr. Young," I said, "this is sacred territory. This is the stove where Ethel made her Christmas lasagna, and that is the table we sat around to eat it. And there is the pantry, where she washed her endless dishes and pans, never letting me help. This chair was hers."

Mr. Young said something very nice. "I can feel her in here, sir."

We walked down the hallway. "Daniel came whizzing down this hallway on a fire truck one Christmas morning and crashed into me. I wasn't ready. My right ankle still bothers me on cold days."

"Is this your office?" he asked, stepping into a room off the hallway.

"Yes, now. It used to be our room. We planned things here in the dark, and talked things over and made decisions. She did most of her wrapping in here on Christmas Eve when the kids were asleep, and she always assigned me to keep watch on the stairs."

He had to leave.

"Will you have something before you go?" I asked him.

"Better not," he said, and then he looked for a long moment at me and said, "Will you have Christmas here?"

"No. I'll go to Steve's house Christmas Eve and Linda's house Christmas Day. There will be a gang at both places."

"Sounds great," he said. "We'll be home, Susan and I and the kids. We do Christmas big, too."

We shook hands and wished each other the best of the season. He said, "Maybe Christmastime is not the best for showing a house. I like it, but I don't think it's what we want."

I surprised myself — but Mr. Young did not seem surprised — when I said, almost without thinking, "Good."

# Nineteen Ninety-Four

*Seen through the woollen eyes of the red angel, the Christmas moment endures. Evermore.*

The red angel can be seen at the top of the tree. This picture was taken in 1983.

## Sometimes It Takes a Dream (about Red) To Open Your Eyes

December 25, 1994

The new silver star I bought for the top of the Christmas tree was a handsome thing. It sparkled in the tree lights as evening closed in.

I finished the trimming. From floor to peak, the tree is about five-and-a-half feet, the shortest ever.

The star was dominating and beautiful. Why then, was I dissatisfied with it? Somehow it didn't fit.

I went to the attic with a flashlight and, after a long search, found the veteran, the red angel. I said, "Come to papa, Red."

She wears a bright red gown with tiny flowers over a conical cardboard frame. Her wings are of the same material with gold backing. Her head is a small Styrofoam ball wrapped tightly with flesh-colored wool. Her eyes, nose, and mouth are sewn on. She has hair of blond wool with a fuzzy gold halo, and she holds a gold hymnbook in pink mittens.

She was dented in the middle and her wings were warped. Her red gown had long ago begun to fade. I made repairs and brought her to the front room and said, "You're outta here, star," and replaced the star with the angel.

I sat in the rocking chair, remembering 36 Christmases in this house. Shortly, the angel spoke to me.

"Turn me more toward the door," she ordered.

I did as she asked, looked her in the eye, and said, "I'm not fearful that you, a piece of cardboard, are talking to me. I'm not even surprised, because I know I'm dreaming. Besides, it's Christmas. By the way, do you ever get frightened way up there?"

She laughed and said, "Are you kidding? After what I've been through? I have looked out from 27 Christmas trees in this house, and I remember many years when my halo brushed the 8-foot ceiling. I have swayed and balanced on unsteady firs and taken a fall with a lot of them. One year I rolled under the couch and wasn't found for 12 hours. One of the babies, Tricia, crawling around, rescued me that year. Remember?"

Of course I remember. I said, "I also remember when you got here. It was 1967. Ever heard the story?"

"Tell me," she said.

"You were an emergency replacement," I said. "You retailed for 39 cents. I bought you on Christmas Eve.

"Luckily, I got home before the stores closed that night, around suppertime. The Christmas aura had settled in. Ethel had made goulash and the nine children — Daniel wasn't here yet — were cleaning their plates and talking about Santa Claus and what he might bring. It was always a magic night.

"Ethel said, 'Look at the top of the tree. The bulb has burned through the middle of the angel. It's ruined.'

"And so it was. The old plastic blue-and-white angel had a holder in the back for a Christmas tree bulb. When the lights were switched on, the angel took on a nice glow and seemed to be floating, wide wings extended.

"'You put it up wrong,' Linda said. She was 10 and Sheila was 9. They were the oldest and often spoke for their brothers and sisters and, I might say, they put no straw 'twixt their teeth.

"I had mounted it improperly. The bulb was touching the plastic. The tree-top symbol was scorched beyond hope.

"The stores were about to close. I rushed off. Ethel said, 'Get an angel, not a star.' You were the last angel, Red. The last one in town, I think.

"You were made in Taiwan. You didn't light up. I think Ethel and the big girls at first thought you were tacky. But you saved another bright Christmas in this house, and you were our angel from then on."

We started reviewing past Christmases, laughing all the way, and then I grew pensive and Red said, "You're thinking of Ethel, aren't you."

I said, "Seven Christmases without her. I'm doing fine, with a good life. I'm happy. The kids and grandkids are great. But sometimes, well, it's a bummer."

She said, "Look at me. I'm 27, old for a Christmas angel. My dress is faded, halo askew, songbook patched, wings warped. And frankly, 5½ feet is plenty high enough for me at this stage.

"Time passes. Things change. And some changes are tough to take. But memories don't change. You went and found me and put me up here because that bright new star, handsome as it is, simply does not belong here. As old and faded as I am, nothing can replace me as long as we are both here. Christmas doesn't change, circumstances change. There is a time for new beginnings. Do those things as bravely as you can, but preserve those things that can never be replaced. You must be careful about that."

She looked at the new star lying nearby and then at me. "Tacky," she said. And then, "Now, wake up from this dream and get with it. You have 16 people coming Christmas Eve."

I woke up, stood up, looked the red angel in the eye, and said aloud, "You've come through for me again, Red."

She made no reply. Cardboard angels only talk to dreamers.

Epilogue

This book, 40 years in the making and 30 in the writing, is complete, with no additions necessary or even possible.

Ethel, her great work done, rests in a lovely country cemetery. The Gallant Ten have long since become adults. While the memories remain in pleasing focus, the era has ended.

The four married kids are making their own family memories on this splendid holiday. The rest, remembering Woodbine Street Christmases, will observe the day each in his or her own special, individual way.

All of us, no matter how widely dispersed, no matter what our circumstances, will look back fondly on at time when the world wore a wide Christmas smile and we were all together. We will remember the aura, Ethel's routines which we followed without question, and, mostly, our warm feelings for each other which were, and continue to be, intensely emphasized on this day.

In the Christmas ahead, and all those to come, I can safely predict that no one will ever be left out. That is the most important element of the legacy; the one wonder of the day which has not given way to time.

It is no longer possible for all of us to gather in one place, even at Christmas. Nor is it desirable. Each family and each individual should, and must, make his or her own Christmas.

But in the course of the day, telephones around the country will be busy wherever a brother or sister is to be found. Every one will speak to every other one, no matter how far away or how busy we are. This is a given. There will be questions like "did you get my gift and does if fit?" There will be laughter and swift reminiscing and "Merry Christmas" at the end of each conversation, said in a way that has unmistakable overtones of eternal familial love and unity.

I am blessed because the "kids" have ceased to be simply my daughters and sons and have, in every true sense, become my friends. I am no longer "Paw." I'm Grandpa, and I have the best possible Christmas situation. There will be a chair for me near a son's or a daughter's tree on Christmas Eve and Christmas morning. And a place at a son's or daughter's table on Christmas Day.

My record will forever remain intact; I will never have a bad Christmas.